IN MY GARDEN

365 Tips for Your
Mid-Atlantic &
New England Garden

Foreword by Liz Ball

Cool Springs Press
Franklin, Tennessee

Published by Cool Springs Press, 101 Forrest Crossing Boulevard,
Franklin, Tennessee 37064

Dunn, Teri. Today in my garden : 365 tips for your Mid-Atlantic &
New England garden / Teri Dunn; foreword by Liz Ball.
p. cm.
ISBN-10: 1-59186-339-2 (pbk.)
ISBN-13: 978-1-59186-339-7
1. Gardening—Mid-Atlantic States. 2. Gardening—New England.
I. Title. II. Title: 365 tips for your Mid-Atlantic & New England garden.

SB451.34.M52D86 2006
635.0975—dc22

2006028073

First Printing: 2006
Printed in Canada
10 9 8 7 6 5 4 3 2 1

Visit the Cool Springs Press website at www.coolspringspress.net.

Never leave that
till tomorrow which
you can do today.

—*Ben Franklin*

CONTENTS

FOREWORD

APPENDIX

❦ EVERYDAY TIP ❦

Get into the habit of keeping a garden
journal. It's like a "baby album" for your
garden. It is invaluable for jotting down
notes about problems or successes,
storing articles from newspapers or
magazines, or attaching photos. It doesn't
have to be fancy, but spiral binding,
tabbed pages, and pockets are convenient.
(It makes a great gift, too!)

FOREWORD

To be a gardener is to be deeply and joyfully in touch will the rhythms of nature. The imperatives of the seasons are constantly evident to us as we feel the soil for moisture, test the air for frost, check the windowsill for sunlight, and glory in each time of the year. Those of us who live in the Mid-Atlantic and New England states—the Northeast—are particularly sensitive to the seasons, because we have four distinctive ones.

The weather cycles deliver predictable cold, then welcome warmth, significant heat, mild chill, then cold again. Each season challenges our understanding of how climate, wildlife, plants, and soil interact as a system in our yards. Each season mandates certain gardening activities, providing structure in our lives and pleasure in the wonder of the natural world.

This handy book is not intended to be a systematic guide, nor is it meant as a chore list to cause you stress because you have not accomplished the suggested gardening activities. *Today in My Garden* is designed to offer timely reminders to busy gardeners of tasks that may bring greater gardening success and enjoyment.

GARDENING IN THE NORTHEAST

We who live in the Mid-Atlantic and New England states enjoy many gardening advantages besides four distinctive seasons. Because our part of the nation was long covered by the huge eastern deciduous forest, which for eons produced multitudes of leaves that decayed into soil, we enjoy generally good, loamy soil that is a bit on the acid side. Recent atypical climate events notwithstanding, we have also traditionally had generous rainfall, distributed fairly evenly over all months of the year.

A look at the USDA cold hardiness zone map reveals that the population centers in states from Pennsylvania and New Jersey north to Maine typically fall within zones 4 to 6. This means that we can grow an enormous variety of plants of all types—trees, shrubs, bulbs, annuals, and perennials. Those that are hardy only in warmer climes, we grow as houseplants! Be sure to check the zone map, found in almost any gardening book, to see exactly what zone you live in. If you choose plants that are listed for that zone or warmer, you should have a good headstart for gardening success.

WORKING TOGETHER

Wherever you garden in the Northeast—mountaintop, valley, plateau, coastal plain—some basic gardening principles apply. They are corollaries of the idea of understanding the natural world and cooperating with it: Work with nature, not against it. Honor and take advantage of the systems for nurture and propagation of plant life that are already in place; after all, they have been successful for ages.

Put the right plant in the right place. Learn your plants' needs and then meet them. Provide the right soil, moisture and light conditions. Give them room to grow to their natural size without your having to prune constantly. This will make them happy and stress free.

Care for the soil so it can care for your plants. Soil is alive. Its organic content— the soft, spongy part called humus— shelters thousands of microscopic fungi, worms, insects, and other organisms that process soil mineral nutrients into a form that plant roots can take up. So, use fertilizers that are safe for soil. These are typically granular products, organic or synthetic, that are labeled "slow-acting" or "slow release." Cover all bare soil to protect it from compaction, drying out, and loss of its "living" organic content. Use organic mulches such as chopped leaves, wood chips, pine needles, or shredded bark. Or, plant living mulches—ground cover plants.

Look for the underlying cause of stress if a plant develops pest or disease problems. Environmental conditions— extreme heat, drought, change in light conditions, soil contamination—often promote stress in plants. People do too, with string trimmers, overuse of chemicals, poor pruning, and other practices. Opportunistic pest and disease organisms are quick to take advantage of plants with impaired defenses. Their presence often signals a deeper an underlying problem

But most important of all is to enjoy today in your garden.

—*Liz Ball*

❧ SPRING ❧

❖ EVERYDAY TIP ❖

If you haven't already
done so, sketch a map of your
garden (it can be simple!)
noting the areas that receive full
sun, a mix of sun and shade,
or full shade. Knowing this is
invaluable to selecting the right
plant, for the right spot.

❧ TIP 1 ❧

Although it's a little early to do a full rosebush pruning, you may attend to winter damage, if any. Go out and trim back obviously dead, snapped, or blackened growth. Be sure to use sharp bypass pruners so that you don't mash or twist the canes as you cut.

☐ *Check when completed*

❖ TIP 2 ❖

Continue to nurture those little
seedlings being raised indoors.
In particular, you should feed them
about every two weeks. Use
a regular, balanced household fertilizer at about fifty percent of the
recommended dilution. This
nudges their growth along and gives
the plants a boost in strength.

❏ *Check when completed*

❧ TIP 3 ❧

If you left your ornamental grasses
to dry last fall and collect snow
over the winter—which always
looks nice—now is the time when
they start to look disreputable.
Chop them down now to make way
for new growth. Cut a few inches
above ground level.

☐ *Check when completed*

✤ TIP 4 ✤

You may now prune your fruit trees, while they are still dormant (that is, before buds show any green). Take out dead and winter-damaged wood, suckers, and branches that rub against one another. Thin the interior so it's not crowded or twiggy, and shape the tree overall.

❏ *Check when completed*

❧ TIP 5 ❧

Watch for snowdrops and early
crocuses. If mulch or lingering snow
is hiding or smothering them,
scrape some of it away so they can
poke their heads up to brighten
the scene. If a late snowstorm
covers them, help them out again
after the weather clears. They're
amazingly resilient.

☐ *Check when completed*

❧ TIP 6 ❧

Order bare-root roses, or buy them locally. These are dormant plants and look like a bundle of twigs, but are actually two-year-old, field-raised plants that the nursery has kept in cold storage over the winter. They often end up being healthier, huskier plants than the potted ones you see later in the season.

☐ *Check when completed*

MARCH

❦ TIP 7 ❦

If you have a cold frame, or
have been thinking of making one,
early spring is the perfect time to
launch it. Little seedlings can be
raised and acclimated in its shelter.
Be sure to water seedlings in the
morning so the foliage has a chance
to dry before evening. Make sure it
has ventilation on sunny days.

 *Check when completed*

❧ TIP 8 ❧

Check on your stored indoor tender bulbs—glads, dahlias, and the like. Get rid of those that show signs of mold or rot, as well as any that are shriveled up. Brush off the dirt; then return the remainder to the storage bags or sacks. Sprinkle on a bit of fungicide powder if rot has been a problem.

❏ *Check when completed*

✤ TIP 9 ✤

Set out a rain barrel. This is a
thrifty way to collect free
water for your garden. You won't
be able to move it later—it
will be too heavy—so choose a spot
where branches or buildings
won't obstruct it, and where
it won't be in the way. Place a
screen over the top to keep out
debris, bugs, dirt, and mosquitos.

☐ *Check when completed*

❧ TIP 10 ❧

Here's an easy way to fulfill an ambitious plan for a splashy bed of annuals ("bedding plants"). Decide what you want, draw up a to-scale plan, and figure out how many plants you will need. Then contact a local nursery with a greenhouse and ask them to grow them just for you. Remember to specify colors.

☐ *Check when completed*

❧ TIP 11 ❧

Take a peek at your pots of overwintered tropical plants. Scoot back
the straw or whatever mulch you
have protecting them; then inspect
the surface of the soil for signs of new
life. If there are sprouts, you may
remove the covering completely and
water lightly. Provide light by placing
them near a window or under
fluorescent lights to encourage them.

☐ *Check when completed*

❧ TIP 12 ❧

Thinking of refurbishing your lawn? Do research now on the kinds most suitable for your region and their conditions (full sun, part-day sun, some shade). Blends are a great way to hedge your bets in varied conditions. When you know what you want, buy bags of seed— or special-order them.

❏ *Check when completed*

❧ TIP 13 ❧

It's time to undertake serious
pruning of your grapevine, while it's
still dormant. This not only keeps
the plant healthy and helps it bear
the best-tasting fruits, but keeps the
harvest within reach. Cut off at least
three-quarters of last season's
growth, chopping all the way back
to a handful of buds per cane.
Sounds harsh, but it pays off!

☐ *Check when completed*

❧ TIP 14 ❧

Once snow has melted, take a walk through the yard with a wheel-barrow or big trash bag. Wear sturdy gloves, carry clippers, and bring a rake. Clean up last year's dead plant material wherever you find it. Also, haul out any debris or fall leaves that blew onto your property over the winter months.

❏ *Check when completed*

❦ TIP 15 ❦

Impatient? Force branches of
flowering shrubs into early bloom.
Cut stems with swelling buds from
forsythia, daphne, willow, flowering
quince, or cornelian cherry. Split
the base of the stems about an inch
to increase water absorption.
Arrange them in lukewarm water
and keep them in a warm room.

❑ *Check when completed*

❧ TIP 16 ❧

Some clematis vines need
to be pruned now—the ones that
you expect to bloom on new growth
when summer arrives. Tug down
last year's tangled, dried-up
growth, cut it away from the plant,
and cart it off. Then simply lop
off all the stems to within a foot or
so of the ground.

☐ *Check when completed*

❧ TIP 17 ❧

Celebrate St. Patrick's Day with your own green carnations! Just buy some white ones, recut their stems, and put them in a vase of water to which you have added several drops of green food coloring. After a few hours, if the color is too light, take out the flowers for a moment, stir in a few more drops of food coloring, and return them to the water.

☐ *Check when completed*

❧ TIP 18 ❧

Keep a close eye on your fruit trees. Before the buds begin to swell, you may spray branch surfaces with dormant (heavy) oil. To be effective, the temperature must be over 45 degrees Fahrenheit. This mainly helps to control scale, but it thwarts other pests, as well.

❏ *Check when completed*

❧ TIP 19 ❧

Shop for new pots. The best
selection is available early, before the
crowds arrive. No matter how
charming a container may be, don't
buy it unless it has at least one
drainage hole. (Alternatively,
perhaps you can nest a smaller pot
within it, or poke or drill a hole
in the bottom.)

☐ *Check when completed*

❧ TIP 20 ❧

Check out the garden soil.
It may still be too soon to plant
much, but it doesn't hurt to
get acquainted. Scoop up a handful
and squeeze. If the dirt oozes
moisture, it's too soon. If it forms a
ball that breaks apart when poked
by your finger, it's okay to sow
early and cold-tolerant crops
(like peas and radishes).

❏ *Check when completed*

❧ TIP 21 ❧

Try "layering" a lower branch on
one of your rhododendrons.
You may just end up with an
additional plant, free and easy.
While it is still attached to the
mother plant, nick the stem, and
then bury that part under the soil.
With luck, new roots will form at
the site of the wound.

❑ *Check when completed*

✤ TIP 22 ✤

Rake the lawn. This gets out any debris, trash, straggling leaves, and weeds from last year. It also helps the grass stand up after months of being matted down, and lets in air and light. All this is conducive to getting your lawn off to a good growing season.

❑ *Check when completed*

✠ TIP 23 ✠

Examine dead patches in the
lawn if it's free of snow or ice. If
they are round and pale yellow
edged in pink, suspect snow mold.
It's a grayish, stringy fungus that
lives under the snow. You may have
to treat the lawn with a fungicide;
ask a lawn service or knowledgeable
staffer at your garden center to
recommend a product.

☐ *Check when completed*

❖ TIP 24 ❖

Groom your perennials as they
emerge from melting snow.
If you didn't cut the tops back last
fall, you should do this now. Tug
out or extract dead stems that are
tangled or collapsed on the
ground. This way, the plants will
have fewer obstacles as they start
up their new season's growth.

❑ *Check when completed*

·TIP 25·

This time of year, if you're walking around in flowerbeds or the vegetable garden, tidying up and making plans, you should be careful. Partially frozen and wet soil is easily compacted or damaged by your footsteps. Lay down some planks to walk on; these redistribute your weight more evenly.

❑ *Check when completed*

❧ TIP 26 ❧

As your spring bulb display
commences, evaluate it.
Did you plant enough? Do you
wish you had more or different
colors? Take notes now, while you're
thinking of it; then tuck those notes
into your calendar or gardening
journal in the late summer or
early fall pages (whenever you are
likely to buy bulbs).

❑ *Check when completed*

❧ TIP 27 ❧

For extra color this time of
year, buy some pansies. They're
wonderfully cold tolerant and
sturdy. Every year seems to bring
more bright new colors and color
combinations—have a little fun
with single-color as well as mix-and-
match displays, in the ground if
it's workable, or in pots.

☐ *Check when completed*

❧ TIP 28 ❧

If late-season snow is in the forecast,
act quickly. Cover vulnerable
plants with plastic, or even blankets
if it's just for the night. Close the
cold frame. Scoop mulch up and
around the bases of perennials.
Spray flowering and fruit trees with
the hose if possible—a coating
of water helps.

❑ *Check when completed*

❧ TIP 29 ❧

Deadhead spent bulb flowers promptly. There's no reason to keep them; if you did, the plants would try to expend valuable energy forming seeds. Plus, removing the flowers keeps your displays looking tidier and fresher longer. A good way to do this is to go out and pick bouquets for the house.

☐ *Check when completed*

❧ TIP 30 ❧

Pre-sprout potatoes so they'll have improved chances of success when you plant them in the ground later on. Choose good, firm ones, free of blemishes and rot. Simply spread them out on a tray—not touching one another. Set the tray in a sunny, warm indoor location.

☐ *Check when completed*

❖ TIP 31 ❖

What's digging up your tulips?
Some sort of hungry little
rodent, no doubt, probably squirrels
or mice (not moles—they're
carnivorous). Gather up survivors
and replant them; then try
sprinkling some smelly dried blood
around the bed or laying evergreen
boughs over the plants until they
are about a foot tall.

☐ *Check when completed*

❖ TIP 32 ❖

Mail-order nurseries that ship bareroot perennials may send your order about now. Always open the package immediately and inspect the contents. Assuming everything looks okay, you may hold them in the fridge or other cold (but not freezing) spot until you are ready to plant them. Sprinkle a little water on them every few days.

❏ *Check when completed*

❧ TIP 33 ❧

Prune deciduous trees and shrubs. They've been dormant all winter and are waking up. Buds are swelling; new growth is just starting. The plants will bounce back from cuts made now because they are so full of energy. Use sharp clippers or loppers. Remove branches that rub together or mar the symmetry or appearance. Thin out interiors.

☐ *Check when completed*

❖ TIP 34 ❖

Prune your rosebushes while
they are still dormant. This is the
time to take out any remaining
damaged canes, as well as crowded
and crossed stems. You may
then shorten undamaged canes in
order to shape the plant—but
never by more than one-third
at any one time.

❑ *Check when completed*

❖ TIP 35 ❖

Always make pruning cuts on an angle. That way, water will be more likely to run off, rather than collecting on the cut area and causing rot or disease. A slanted cut also dries out faster after a rain. Last but not least, this leaves a smaller stub, which is better for a plant's appearance.

☐ *Check when completed*

❧ TIP 36 ❧

Evaluate the shape of your
needled evergreens. If there are
branches jutting out at odd
angles, early spring is a good time to
get rid of them. Don't just shorten
them as much as needed, or you'll
be left looking at an ugly stub.
Instead, prune down low, within the
plant, and no one will be the wiser.

❏ *Check when completed*

❦ TIP 37 ❦

As any remaining snow melts and
the yard comes to life, clear out
the lawn, flowerbeds, and vegetable
garden before you get too busy
and before plant growth covers
everything. Get rid of rocks that
may have risen to the soil surface;
rake out gravel and sand that might
have been shoveled or pushed in.

☐ *Check when completed*

❧ TIP 38 ❧

Thinking of moving a shrub or small tree to a new location? Early spring is a great time to do this, while the plant is still dormant (so it won't be traumatized). When it does start growing, it can direct all its energy into a great show. Just be sure the soil is workable before undertaking this project.

❏ *Check when completed*

❧ TIP 39 ❧

Get in the habit of forming a
basin around every plant you
install or move. It should
be around the perimeter of the
plant's canopy "drip line" (the outer
edge). Mound soil up a few
inches in a circle around the plant's
root zone. Then, when you water,
it will go straight to the roots. A
basin also holds mulch well.

❑ *Check when completed*

❧ TIP 40 ❧

Make a holding or "nursery" area in
a sheltered part of your yard.
Clear it out, define its boundaries
with a low fence or some rocks,
and put in some organic matter. You
can temporarily plant ("heel in")
bare-root shrubs, trees, and
rosebushes here until they are ready
to go into their permanent home.

❏ *Check when completed*

❧ TIP 41 ❧

Are deer an ongoing problem?
Their destructive dining can be even
more frustrating this time of year,
when they go after young, emerging
plants or ones you've just installed.
Various repellents can work, but if
those deer are relentless and you
mean business, you need an 8-foot-
tall fence around your garden.

☐ *Check when completed*

❧ TIP 42 ❧

Trim your evergreen hedge before it really starts growing for the year. Remove old stems at their bases. Shorten others that are too long. Shape so that the top of the plant—when viewed from the side—is narrower than the base. This not only looks better but is easier to maintain.

❏ *Check when completed*

❧ TIP 43 ❧

Be on the lookout for seedling
trees. They can pop up anywhere in
the yard, but are a problem where
you've put a mulch of chopped-up
fall leaves. These pests can elbow
out plants you want, while hogging
water and soil nutrients. It's tedious,
but you'd best yank them out or cut
them down with a sharp hoe.

☐ *Check when completed*

❧ TIP 44 ❧

Spring is a fine time to remove a tree limb. Assuming it's not too thick or too high up, you can do this yourself with a good sharp handsaw. Use the three-cuts method: an undercut halfway up; an overcut a bit farther out and halfway down (at this point, the branch snaps right off); then a neat final cut at the collar to finish.

❑ *Check when completed*

❧ TIP 45 ❧

Want to rejuvenate your thin-stemmed rhubarb? Here's what to do. Every three or four years, when the first buds emerge, dig up, divide, and replant the clumps. Feed the transplanted pieces with a high-nitrogen fertilizer now and then intermittently over the summer. (Then resist doing any harvesting until the next year.)

❑ *Check when completed*

❖ TIP 46 ❖

Photograph your spring bulb
displays when they are at their best.
It's fun to admire what you've done,
but there is a practical benefit, as
well. You can refer to these photos
in the fall, when you may want to
improve or revise the show and need
help remembering what was
growing where.

❏ *Check when completed*

❧ TIP 47 ❧

If snowfall has been light over the winter months, the ground may be rather dry deep down. So once you are sure the soil has thawed, haul out the hose and soak your shrubs and evergreens. This rehydrates their root systems and will help them get off to a good start.

☐ *Check when completed*

❧ TIP 48 ❧

Now is the time to start removing
winter mulch—compost, straw,
salt-marsh hay, some other organic
material, whatever you laid down
last fall—from your flowerbeds.
Wait until the air temperatures are
consistently at or above freezing.
Remove it gradually. Use your
hands, a rake, a leaf blower, even
some strong blasts from the hose.

❏ *Check when completed*

❧ TIP 49 ❧

Plants you've ordered by
mail that arrive in pots must be
unpacked right away. Remove
all packing material, plastic wrap,
and soil collars, and give them a
good soaking. If you're not
ready to plant them, just keep
them in a cool, sheltered spot
for up to a week or so.

❑ *Check when completed*

❧ TIP 50 ❧

To plant bare-root perennials,
wait until the ground outside is
workable and not soggy. Dig a
generous hole, scoop in some
organic matter, and scrape the
sides—all this is to help the
roots establish themselves in their
new home. Set plants at the same
level they were growing in the
pot, backfill, and water well.

❑ *Check when completed*

❧ TIP 51 ❧

Protect newly planted perennials
from sun and wind. Some
judiciously placed lawn chairs can
help, as can cardboard boxes,
pieces of plywood, or polyspun row
cover fabric. The idea is to shelter
the plants and keep them warm
while they try to adjust and "get
their legs under them."

❑ *Check when completed*

❧ TIP 52 ❧

Are you growing edible fruit trees,
like plum or peach? Have you
noticed the crops for some years
are big, and other years are
disappointing? Early spring is the
perfect time to intervene to make
things more even and predictable. If
this is a good year, thin the fruits.
Pick off and dispose of half the
fruit while it is still tiny.

☐ *Check when completed*

❧ TIP 53 ❧

Try raising your own salad mix!
Seed companies call these blends
"mesclun," and they often contain a
range of lettuces, as well as other
tasty edible leafy greens. Sow in
moist, well-drained soil, and lay
down a row cover (it shields them
from a late frost, plant pests, and
hot sun). They grow rapidly.

❑ *Check when completed*

❧ TIP 54 ❧

Manage your mint. This tasty herb,
unfortunately, starts to grow
rampantly as the soil warms up. So
act early. Dig up and discard sprouts
growing where you don't want
them. Confine the rest in a
bottomless plastic container (such as
a gallon milk jug), pushed down
into the ground around the clump.

❏ *Check when completed*

❦ TIP 55 ❦

Buy a watering wand. It attaches
to the end of a hose and delivers
a softer, soaking spray that is ideal
for watering seedlings and new
transplants without knocking
them over. Look for one that has a
handy thumb-operated on-off valve.
Some models have several settings,
so you can choose from mist,
gentle shower, or jet spray.

❑ *Check when completed*

❧ TIP 56 ❧

If you are planting a peony (or other bushy perennial), or have one that is just emerging, set a peony ring over it sooner rather than later. This metal support—available in garden centers and from mail-order sources—prevents flopping, and better displays the gorgeous, heavy-headed blossoms. The growing plant will hide the support.

❑ *Check when completed*

❧ TIP 57 ❧

Protect small plants from weather
or pests with "cloches." You can buy
fancy glass or plastic models but
homemade ones work fine. A
gallon plastic milk jug is a favorite,
as are plastic soda bottles. Cut off
one end and push it into the
ground over the plant. Cloches of
any kind also keep your plants
a bit warmer, a nice plus.

☐ *Check when completed*

❧ TIP 58 ❧

If a deer fence is not practical
for your yard, you may have some
luck discouraging deer with repellents. You'll find plenty of spray
products sold for this purpose.
They ought to be replenished after
a rain. Or suspend—on string
or twine—bars of scented soap from
branches. (Irish Spring and
Lifebuoy are particularly intense.)

❏ *Check when completed*

❧ TIP 59 ❧

If you have not done so yet,
fertilize your rhododendrons when
they are blooming. Because they
prefer acidic soil growing
conditions, use a slow-acting
fertilizer especially intended for
them. Follow the instructions about
amount on the label. If you water
the plants before and after feeding,
the dose will be most effective.

☐ *Check when completed*

❧ TIP 60 ❧

Tuck some colorful annuals in and
among your bulbs. If you do this
while the bulbs are in bloom, not
only does the display look brighter,
but also you won't inadvertently
be digging into the bulbs or their
root systems when you add flowers
later. Good companions include
pansies and primroses. They hide
the dying bulb foliage, too.

❑ *Check when completed*

❧ TIP 61 ❧

When picking daffodils for
bouquets, cut a long piece of stem.
Once inside, though, do some
trimming. There's a pale green or
white section at the very base of
every stem; this should be cut off, as
it won't take up water. One other
thing—pick only a few from each
clump, so you can still enjoy
an outdoor display.

☐ *Check when completed*

❧ TIP 62 ❧

Tidy perennial beds. Once the
mulch layer is off, go into the
garden with a pair of clippers. Cut
all remaining dead stalks from
last fall down to the crown of the
plant. As you work, tread carefully—
if the ground is still semi-frozen
or saturated with water, your
footsteps can compact the soil.

❏ *Check when completed*

❖ TIP 63 ❖

Spread compost. Whether store-bought or homemade, it is always beneficial for your garden, especially early in the season. Because compost is sometimes still decomposing, it generates some heat, a hedge against springtime's temperature swings. Sprinkle to a depth of 1 to 3 inches, broadcasting it by hand, or with a trowel or shovel.

❑ *Check when completed*

❧ TIP 64 ❧

Install edging around beds and
lawn areas. Take a look at the
choices at the home-supply store or
garden center: metal, brick,
cedar shakes, plastic, concrete, and
stone. Whatever you decide,
it's a good idea to dig a trench. This
not only defines your line and
holds the edging, but should help
keep encroaching plants at bay.

❏ *Check when completed*

❧ TIP 65 ❧

After danger of frost is past and soil has warmed, you may plant your summer bulbs—such as dahlias, galtonias, and glads. These like organically rich, well-drained soil and a spot with plenty of sunshine. Also, assuming you are growing the tall kinds, place them where they won't block other plants from view.

❏ *Check when completed*

✤ TIP 66 ✤

Deadhead—that is, clip spent blooms off your spring-blooming shrubs (such as lilacs, spirea, rhododendrons, and azaleas). Be careful and thorough; get the back of the plant, and use a ladder or chair to get high flowers. Deadheading helps the plants conserve energy; plus they look a lot better.

❏ *Check when completed*

❧ TIP 67 ❧

Buy some ear plugs. Garden equipment that you will soon be using—whether lawn mower, rototiller, or chainsaw—is noisy. Indeed, some machines can hit 100 decibels, which is harmful if we subject ourselves to the din repeatedly. Wearing protection is also a nice way to signal that you want to be left alone to concentrate on your work!

☐ *Check when completed*

❦ TIP 68 ❦

Leave fading bulb foliage to
receive sun so it can send nutrients
to fuel next year's show down into
the bulb below. The leaves will
yellow and flop, and no, the
process isn't pretty. Bending over
handfuls and cinching them with a
rubber band has no benefits, though
it may look slightly better.

❑ *Check when completed*

❧ TIP 69 ❧

Don't rush a corn planting—the
seeds languish or even rot in cold,
damp ground. Wait until the
soil has warmed up. Plant an inch
or two deep; shallower plantings
tend to sprout faster because
they are nearer to the ground
surface, which is warmer. Always
sow more than you think you'll
need; you can thin later.

❑ *Check when completed*

❧ TIP 70 ❧

If a bed or vegetable garden has
not yet been planted, try some
preemptive weed control. Cover the
area with black plastic, and
weigh down the edges with rocks or
bricks. Leave the plastic in
place as long as you can. Weeds are
among the first plants to
sprout in spring, and this suffocates
many of them early on.

❏ *Check when completed*

❖ TIP 71 ❖

Damp spring? This means mosquitoes will soon be out in force, making yard work miserable. Do what you can now to prevent a population explosion. Dump out or upend pots, tires, and other water-holding areas. Toss soil or sand over puddles. Add guppies to a garden pool—the fish will dine on mosquito larvae before they can hatch.

❏ *Check when completed*

❧ TIP 72 ❧

If you've been meaning to get a
clematis, springtime is ideal because
plants are typically sold bare root
and dormant. Choose a bright spot,
with moist, fertile soil. After planting, mulch the base with several
inches of compost or other organic
matter, because clematis roots like to
be moist and shaded. Install a
support or trellis at planting time.

❏ *Check when completed*

❧ TIP 73 ❧

Little groundcover plants are for
sale now. But do your homework—
is your intended site sunny or
shady? Do you want something that
flowers? Then prepare the spot,
clearing it out and adding organic
matter. Don't set the plants too close
together; they will fill in. In the
meantime, lay down mulch to keep
the soil moist and prevent weeds.

❑ *Check when completed*

❖ TIP 74 ❖

Start "hardening off" seedlings you've raised indoors. This means gradually adjusting them to outdoor conditions. Put them in a somewhat sheltered spot, keep them watered, and bring them back inside if a late frost threatens. (If you instead move them straight from the house into the ground, they really struggle, so don't skip this step.)

❏ *Check when completed*

❧ TIP 75 ❧

It's easy to plant a small tree or shrub; you can do it before lunch. Dig an ample hole. Have some organic amendments on hand to mix with the native soil for shrubs. (Trees need ordinary soil.) Set the plant into the hole, check that it's straight and is above soil level. Then backfill and tamp the soil down gently. Water well and mulch.

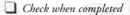 ☐ *Check when completed*

❧ TIP 76 ❧

Once your spring-flowering
shrubs are finished blooming, you
may go out and prune and shape
them. Don't wait too long; they
will soon start developing buds for
next year's show, and you don't
want to trim those off. Now is the
time. While you're at it, do some
thinning—the plants will look
better and be healthier as a result.

❑ *Check when completed*

❧ TIP 77 ❧

A containerized rose can be planted
anytime from mid- to late spring.
Dig a hole bigger than the pot, and
have some extra organic matter
ready to add to it as you plant.
Ease the rose out, and loosen dense
roots with your fingers. Replant at
the same level it was in the pot,
water well and mulch.

❏ *Check when completed*

❧ TIP 78 ❧

Fertilize your shrubs throughout
the yard. Use a balanced slow-acting
granular fertilizer for nursery
plants for consistent nutrition over
several months. It's a good idea to
soak the plants, right at their bases,
before and after, so the food reaches
the roots. (This isn't as necessary if
the weather has been rainy.)

❑ *Check when completed*

❧ TIP 79 ❧

The first time to feed your
roses is after they have already leafed
out and flower buds are
beginning to swell and show a bit
of color. Special fertilizers are
sold for roses, but you can
also use an all-purpose, slow-acting
granular formula. Scratch it into
the soil and water it in.

☐ *Check when completed*

❧ TIP 80 ❧

Repair your lawn chairs! First,
remove any broken or frayed
webbing. Then buy a roll of nylon
webbing at the hardware store—
matching it in terms of width and
color. Cut it to length, weave it
through the existing bands, and fold
the ends to reinforce the pressure
points. Then secure the ends
with snug-fitting screws.

❑ *Check when completed*

❧ TIP 81 ❧

A big pot need not be super-heavy.
Don't fill it completely with
potting soil when the plants within
use only a few inches' worth.
Instead, put a layer of foam peanuts
in the bottom first. Nobody will
know, the plants will be fine, and
you'll be able to pick up the pot and
move it if you want.

☐ *Check when completed*

❖ TIP 82 ❖

If your area's last frost date has passed
and the soil temperature is above
50 degrees F., you can set out tomato
seedlings, in the ground or in tubs or
pots. If the weather is cooler, drape
plastic over them overnight or use a
Wall-o-Water™. Set plants a little
deeper than they were in the pot or
flat—new roots will develop from the
stems and help anchor them.

❏ *Check when completed*

❧ TIP 83 ❧

Aerating can improve compacted soil under your grass. Rent a core-aerating machine to punch 3-inch holes into the grass, and to pull up the plugs of soil at regular intervals. This lets water and air into the soil. As the soil cores dissolve over the next few rains, organisms in the soil regenerate and turfgrass improves.

❑ *Check when completed*

❧ TIP 84 ❧

Decorate a lamppost! Wrap it
with a 4-foot-tall, slender piece of
chicken wire, overlapping the ends
and cinching them tightly in place
(use wire cutters rather than your
fingers—it's easier on your hands).
Then plant a climbing vine right at
the base. By midsummer, foliage
and flowers will hide the wire and
the post will be a pretty sight.

❏ *Check when completed*

❧ TIP 85 ❧

Divide overgrown perennials, ones
in large clumps, or ones that seem
to be less productive every
year. Dig up the clumps and divide
into sections. Discard the centers
and save the outer sections—making
sure each piece has a good clump
of roots and some emerging
green growth. Replant, evenly
spaced, and water well.

☐ *Check when completed*

❖ TIP 86 ❖

Got dandelions? Don't let
them go to seed! Even if you lack
the time and energy to dig up each
plant by the roots (remember, these
have very long taproots), at least
remove the furry yellow flowers
before they become white balls of
drifting seeds. A pass of the
lawnmower should do the trick.

❏ *Check when completed*

❧ TIP 87 ❧

Start a strawberry patch in a
sunny site. Since strawberries have
shallow roots, the soil should be
loose and free of rocks to a depth of
several inches. Add a couple of
inches of organic matter, then plant.
Allow each plant about a square
foot of space; set the crown just
above the soil line.

❏ *Check when completed*

❧ TIP 88 ❧

Weed with a sharp hoe. It's a quick
and easy way to dispatch a
crowd of young weeds, which is
what you get this time of year. Keep
your strokes shallow, though—
you don't want to harm the roots of
the desirable plants or bring more
weed seeds to the surface.

❑ *Check when completed*

❧ TIP 89 ❧

Fill a windowbox. First make sure any remnants of last year's show have been scraped out. Put in fresh potting soil. Arrange the pots of plants atop the soil first, and shift them around if you wish—sort of a dress rehearsal. Then plant them at the level they were in the pot, add slow-acting granular fertilizer, and water thoroughly.

❑ *Check when completed*

❖ TIP 90 ❖

Do poppies make poor bouquet
flowers? Not true! It's just
that sap dripping from the cut ends
fouls vase water. Use the florist
trick. Pick them in their full glory
(or slightly before) and seal
the cut ends: Dip them in boiling
water for 30 seconds, or singe
the ends with a candle or match.

❑ *Check when completed*

❧ EVERYDAY TIP ❧

Enjoy your garden.
In the midst of chores and
to-do lists, you might overlook
why it's such a pleasure. Sit outside,
read a book, take a stroll, snooze
in a hammock, have a
party—reap the rewards.

❧ TIP 91 ❧

Plant some annuals now that both air and soil are warm enough. But avoid the temptation to buy blooming plants—the transition from their pampered life at the garden center to your yard may cause them to drop their petals. They'll recover, of course, but it's smarter to buy annuals with plenty of good buds.

☐ *Check when completed*

❧ TIP 92 ❧

Keep watering your small
transplants. Remember: Too much
water and the roots will rot, but too
little and they will be stressed—
possibly to the point of death. Water
to soak the soil, and let it dry
out between waterings. Morning is
the best time to water.

❑ *Check when completed*

❧ TIP 93 ❧

Head off lawn-mowing challenges
by displaying your birdbath, sun-
dial, garden bench, or other
décor up on paving blocks. Seat the
paver securely in the ground.
Don't forget to check that it's level
(this is particularly important
if you are using more than one to
support a single item).

❑ *Check when completed*

❧ TIP 94 ❧

Zap weeds in the cracks of your
sidewalk, walkway, patio, or
driveway, one by one, safely. Just fill
a spray bottle with white vinegar
(with a few drops of dish soap to
contribute stickiness) and hit
each one with a strong blast. If the
weed isn't dead in a day, spray it
again . . . it should succumb.

❏ *Check when completed*

❧ TIP 95 ❧

Keep cats from treating your
flowerbeds like a litter box! One way
to do this is to lay down some
chicken wire and cover it lightly
with soil or mulch—they don't like
the way their paws get snagged.
Alternatively, try sprinkling an
unpleasant-smelling repellent
around: hot pepper, black pepper,
citronella oil, even coffee grounds.

❑ *Check when completed*

❖ TIP 96 ❖

Pull weeds out by the roots. They compete with your plants, especially the new and smaller ones, hogging valuable resources of soil nutrients, water, and sunlight. Often they harbor insects and plant diseases, too. Note that it is much easier to get out the entire weed when the ground is damp, after a rain or shortly after you've watered.

❏ *Check when completed*

☙ TIP 97 ❧

Remove diseased, infested, or
dead leaves from ornamental plants
whenever you see them. Don't
let them just fall off and hang
around the base of your plants,
where they can harbor and
encourage problems. Get that stuff
out—way out. Don't even toss it
on your compost pile. Send it away
with the household garbage.

❏ *Check when completed*

❧ TIP 98 ❧

Cut back stems of young mum
plants by one-third, now and in July.
Though it seems brutal, this
operation causes them to grow
shorter but bushier (left alone,
they can get leggy and fall over).
They will bloom a bit later as a
result, but the plants will stronger
and at their peak in fall.

❏ *Check when completed*

❧ TIP 99 ❧

Time to remind your forsythia bush who's boss! Once all the flowers have faded, the branches will elongate like crazy until the plant is way out of bounds. While this is not a plant for a clipped and formal look, it will look better (and grow more densely) with an early summer haircut. Use sharp pruners and cut individual branches for a natural shape.

☐ *Check when completed*

❧ TIP 100 ❧

Mulch around the bases of your perennials, or renew depleted mulch. The weather's getting warmer now, and the soil dries out faster; a good mulch layer really helps retain moisture. Be careful, however, not to push the mulch flush up against the stems or crown of the plants and trees, which can invite rot.

☐ *Check when completed*

❖ TIP 101 ❖

If you weren't happy with the
location or numbers of some of your
spring bulbs, it is safe to dig
them up and move them elsewhere
in the yard. Their foliage should
have died down by now, or nearly
so, and thus they should be
practically dormant—an optimum
time to make your move.

☐ *Check when completed*

❧ TIP 102 ❧

Like your evergreens neat? Trim
now, clip or shear back new growth
(the candles, in the case of pines)
before it is fully expanded. Don't
make severe cuts, just shaping ones,
at this time. This also helps keep
evergreens in bounds and inspires
them to grow more densely.

❑ *Check when completed*

❧ TIP 103 ❧

Check on established vines as
well as ones you planted this year.
Most are surging into growth.
If you don't intervene sooner rather
than later, and direct the stems
where you want them to go, the
whole display can get out of
control pretty quickly. Train and tie
elongating branches onto their
support with strips of soft cloth.

☐ *Check when completed*

❖ TIP 104 ❖

When watering shrubs, rosebushes,
and trees, a slow, deep soaking is
better than occasional lighter sprink-
lings. Set the hose at the base of the
plant, at a slow trickle, and come
back in an hour or so. Check with a
trowel or a houseplant water meter
probe to see if moisture has pene-
trated several inches. If not, water for
another hour or until you are satisfied.

❏ *Check when completed*

❧ TIP 105 ❧

Patch bare spots in your lawn. Rake debris and then broadcast perennial ryegrass seed as evenly as you can. Sprinkle a dusting of slow-acting granular lawn fertilizer, then a thin layer of soil over the seeds. Water gently with a sprinkler today, and daily until the grass has sprouted and is growing well.

❑ *Check when completed*

❖ TIP 106 ❖

Tall-growing perennials often benefit from staking—foxgloves, hollyhocks, verbascums, penstemons, and delphiniums, to name a few. If you didn't insert a wooden or metal support at planting time, it's probably not too late. Just poke the support securely into the ground close by, and attach the plant to it at intervals with soft ties.

❑ *Check when completed*

❧ TIP 107 ❧

Spend some time grooming
your annuals, whether they are
growing in pots, in a windowbox,
or in the ground. Remove spent
flowers, and pinch off yellowing or
damaged leaves. This not only helps
the plants look nicer, but keeps
them healthier and inspires
continued bloom production.

❑ *Check when completed*

❧ TIP 108 ❧

Nip insect-pest problems early.
When you see harmful bugs or
beetles dining on your flowers or in
your vegetable garden, handpick and
toss them in a bucket of soapy
water. If you don't know their identity, look them up in a gardening
book or show a sample to someone
knowledgeable so you can learn
how to fight off infestations.

❏ *Check when completed*

❧ TIP 109 ❧

Move potted houseplants
outside to a patio or deck for the
summer months. The fresh
air and bright sunshine will do them
good. But make the transition
gradual. If they get too much sun at
first, you'll observe brown patches
on the leaves which is, yes, sunburn.
Better to set them in part-day sun at
first and see how they do.

☐ *Check when completed*

❧ TIP 110 ❧

Pick some edible flowers
(unsprayed, of course) for a summer
meal! Chives, nasturtiums, and
pansies can all go in a salad.
You can mix calendula petals or
lavender flowers in soft butter for a
unique, tasty spread for bread
or crackers. Rose petals and bee balm
blossoms are a pretty addition
to a fruit punch.

❑ *Check when completed*

❧ TIP III ❧

Create a focal-point planting. First, select a big, dramatic, or unusual pot or urn. To make it stand out further, elevate it on a support (a pedestal, overturned pot, or stack of bricks). Then fill it with enough plants so that it can be admired from any angle. Pick colors that contrast with the surroundings so it automatically captures attention.

☐ *Check when completed*

❧ TIP 112 ❧

Spruce up dull plantings with plants
that have colorful leaves. These will
maintain garden excitement even as
flowers around them cycle in and out
of bloom. Some good choices are
caladium, coral-bells, coleus,
elephant's ear, sweet potato vine, and
tricolor sage. Variegated-leaved
geraniums, lamium, nasturtiums,
and ivy can also do the trick.

☐ *Check when completed*

❖ TIP 113 ❖

Make a mini water garden in
a tub or kettle. It must be 18 inches
deep to host a potted water lily (ask
the nursery about ones that do well
in smaller quarters). Or try other
attractive aquatics, both floaters and
tall ones like irises, papyrus, and
taro. Full sun is best. Top off the
water when it evaporates a bit.

☐ *Check when completed*

❧ TIP 114 ❧

When weather starts to get hotter,
watering often, and enough,
can become a real chore. Get some
soaker hoses and thread them
through the flowerbeds, groundcover area, vegetable garden,
or any other spot that needs regular
moisture. For these, as well as for
sprinklers, consider investing in a
timer that installs at the faucet.

❑ *Check when completed*

❧ TIP 115 ❧

Improve hose-watering in
general. First of all, you get what
you pay for—cheap hoses
crack and leak after a while. Spend a
little more on a rubber hose, or a
"professional duty" nylon/PVC
model. Buy some hose guides so
you don't drag the hose over plants.
And always store your hose inside,
or at least in the shade.

☐ *Check when completed*

❧ TIP 116 ❧

Mow the lawn less often during
dry weather spells. When you do
mow, set the mower blades higher to
help keep the grass green and allow
grass blades to shade out low-
growing weeds. (Taller types tend to
develop deeper roots.) Don't bother
with raking—if you mow often,
the clippings will be small enough
to break down on site.

❏ *Check when completed*

❧ TIP 117 ❧

Algae problem in your
birdbath? Assuming you've cleaned
it (a mixture of equal parts of
vinegar and water works well and is
nontoxic for the birds), there's one
other thing you can try. Pick about
six stems off your lavender plant,
wrap them with a rubber band, and
float the bundle in the water.

☐ *Check when completed*

❧ TIP 118 ❧

Deadhead both annuals and perennials. That is, pinch or cut off spent flowers promptly. Otherwise, the plants may be tempted to spend a lot of energy going to seed and the flower show will end. This way, you persuade them to redirect their energy into making a fresh round of flowers.

☐ *Check when completed*

❧ TIP 119 ❧

Remember your hanging baskets!
In warm summer weather, they
dry out amazingly quickly. Use a
watering wand and soak thoroughly
in the mornings. A "mulch" of
damp moss, an inch or so thick,
arrayed over the soil surface helps
retain moisture between waterings.
Just scoot it aside when watering
and reposition it after.

☐ *Check when completed*

❧ TIP 120 ❧

Have your marigolds turned to lace?
If so, suspect slugs. Go on
a night safari to see what's eating
them. If it is slugs, try the
beer trick. Place a shallow dish
filled with stale beer by the
plants; by morning, any slugs
attracted to the beer will be
drowned or too drunk to care.

❏ *Check when completed*

❖ TIP 121 ❖

Pick bouquets often! It's one
of the great rewards of gardening;
plus the very process of going out
and selecting flowers compels you
to examine—and enjoy—your
plants as you go by. Bring a water
bucket and plunk in the stems as
you go. This keeps everything fresh
until you get inside, where you can
groom and shorten each stem.

❏ *Check when completed*

❖ TIP 122 ❖

If you haven't already, clip
off all spent, browned lilac flowers.
They really detract from the
appearance of the plant, and they
drain energy from it as they attempt
to go to seed. If you don't do
this, they'll hang around all summer
and all winter and detract from
next spring's glorious purple
or white show.

❏ *Check when completed*

❧ TIP 123 ❧

For July Fourth, make a patriotic flower display. Get some red or blue pots. Then fill the red ones with blue and white annuals, and the blue ones with red and white flowers. Group them together—on the front steps to welcome visitors or to the side on the patio or deck— where they can be admired.

☐ *Check when completed*

❧ TIP 124 ❧

In your shade garden, as the
ground gets drier, bleeding heart,
corydalis, and other early-flowering
perennials tend to throw in the towel.
Flowering is done, and the stems and
leaves start to yellow. There is no
reason to watch and wait. Take sharp
clippers and cut everything down to the
ground. Don't worry; the plants will
return in glory next spring.

❑ *Check when completed*

❖ TIP 125 ❖

Beat the heat for your potted
plants. Hard surfaces such as the
patio, deck, or steps absorb a
lot of solar energy (especially dark
or brick surfaces), which is radiated
back with a vengeance and can
literally bake your plants. Watering
helps, but you may also have to
temporarily move pots to the edges
or to somewhat shadier settings.

❑ *Check when completed*

❧ TIP 126 ❧

Keep after those weeds!
Knock down carpets of smaller ones
with a hoe—make sure it's sharp,
and it will do an impressive
job. Otherwise, hand-pull individual
ones. Work in the morning
hours, if you can, so you don't get
overheated (evening may be full
of swarming mosquitoes).

❏ *Check when completed*

❧ TIP 127 ❧

Visit the garden center for
midsummer bargains. The crowds
are gone, and the offerings may be
depleted, but sometimes you can
score good deals on larger plants.
Just remember that anything you
plant now will need extra water and
attention to survive the stress of
being moved in the heat.

☐ *Check when completed*

❖ TIP 128 ❖

Lift up and look under your
potted plants. If the contents have
been thriving, roots may have
filled the entire container and be
clogging the drainage holes.
If water cannot drain properly,
performance declines and rot can
follow. Two solutions: repot the
contents in something larger, or
remove a plant or two.

❑ *Check when completed*

❧ TIP 129 ❧

Sketch or photograph your flowerbeds when they are at their peak. Not only will the images be a source of pride, but they'll also provide useful information when you view them with care later. You'll be able to identify successful combinations, as well as ones that didn't work out—all fodder for deciding on next year's plans.

❑ *Check when completed*

❧ TIP 130 ❧

Japanese beetles? These half-inch,
metallic, green-and-copper pests
make some gardeners homicidal.
Just a few can decimate a rose planting; plus they attack other garden
flowers. Spread a cloth under
the affected plants, shake the plants
to dislodge the beetles, then scoop
them up and drown them in a
bucket of soapy water.

☐ *Check when completed*

❖ TIP 131 ❖

Berry plants will soon start to ripen their sweet harvest. But there's competition for the fruit—birds, wild animals, and various insect pests. Luckily, they can all be thwarted the same way—if you act early. Drape the plants in netting; garden-supply shops and mail-order suppliers sell large-enough pieces with the right mesh.

☐ *Check when completed*

❧ TIP 132 ❧

Visit the shrubs, rosebushes, and
trees that you planted this
spring and give each one a tune-up.
(You should already be supplying
good soaking waterings.) Check for
signs of disease and insect pests.
Cut off all afflicted plant parts and
get rid of them. (But save a small
amount if you need a diagnosis
and advice on treatment.)

❑ *Check when completed*

❧ TIP 133 ❧

Time to give rampant-growing
shrubs and hedges another haircut!
Use freshly sharpened clippers and
loppers. If the plants are thorny or
twiggy, wear a long-sleeved shirt
and tough gloves as you work.
Remove suckers emerging from the
bases. Clip back new growth all
around to inspire a thicker profile.

☐ *Check when completed*

❧ TIP 134 ❧

Some plants develop powdery
mildew in midsummer, thanks to
the heat and humidity. In particular,
the leaves of lilacs, roses, phlox, and
green beans turn powdery white.

There's not much you can do,
save trying to improve air circulation within and around the plants
with a little judicious clipping. In
the future, plant resistant varieties.

❏ *Check when completed*

❦ TIP 135 ❦

If your area experiences a prolonged hot or dry spell, refrain from fertilizing. Fertilizer is most effective when plants are well hydrated and their soil is damp; otherwise, the food never reaches the roots or can "burn" them. Also, freshly fed plants tend to put on a flush of new growth, which would be instantly stressed by the blazing weather.

❏ *Check when completed*

❧ TIP 136 ❧

Keep pots of herbs near the
kitchen for spontaneous summer
meals. Ones that do well in a
container include rosemary, cilantro,
sage, parsley, oregano, chives, and
thyme. Water in the morning and
cut just before using for best flavor.
Rinse off dust or dirt before using.
Cut herbs often to prevent flowering,
which changes foliage flavor.

❏ *Check when completed*

❧ TIP 137 ❧

Float rose petals in a punch or
sangria, or scatter them over butter-
cream-frosted cake or cupcakes. Pick
them on a hot afternoon when the
fragrance is at its peak; rinse them
gently (critically important if you have
sprayed your rosebushes; unsprayed
flowers are safest), pat dry, then store
in a plastic bag in the refrigerator for
a few hours before using.

☐ *Check when completed*

❧ TIP 138 ❧

Here's a clever way to water hanging
baskets or other potted plants,
especially when you won't be around
to attend to them on a hot day. Set
a few ice cubes on their surface
before you leave the house. These
will melt slowly over the course of
a few hours, gradually soaking in.

❏ *Check when completed*

❧ TIP 139 ❧

Lower leaves of your tomato plants
turning yellow? This is caused
by plant diseases that develop in hot
weather when air circulation is poor.
If the plant is not too bushy yet,
installing a tomato cage may help
improve air circulation. Also be sure
to water right at ground level; never
let water splash up onto the leaves.

☐ *Check when completed*

❖ TIP 140 ❖

Check on your compost pile.
Hot weather causes the contents to
break down faster, and you may
find you have a bounty of "black
gold." If you don't use it, it will
continue to break down. Instead,
scoop it out and use it around
the yard as a nourishing mulch on
heat-stressed plants.

☐ *Check when completed*

❧ TIP 141 ❧

If you are growing leafy herbs
for harvest, prevent them from
going to seed by pinching off
flowers when they develop. This
forces the plants to continue
producing tasty leaves and prevents
self-sowing. Last but not least, it
thwarts bees, which are more
interested in the flowers than any
other part of the plant, of course.

☐ *Check when completed*

❧ TIP 142 ❧

As soon as flowers or stems start
to turn brown, cut them back
to live growth. This not only
improves their appearance, but helps
prevent insect pests and diseases
from moving in. And it will
encourage some plants to rebloom
later in the season. Cut-and-come-
again favorites include yarrow,
daisies, and delphiniums.

☐ *Check when completed*

❧ TIP 143 ❧

Look before you squish a garden
bug! Not all are harmful pests.
When in doubt as to a critter's
identity, look him up in gardening
books or take one (in a jar) to a
garden center staffer. If it is a pest,
you can get advice on how to
combat it and buy any product you
might need while there.

☐ *Check when completed*

❧ TIP 144 ❧

Weed-whacking is not a fun chore, but these tips will make the project faster and more efficient. If possible, work in the late afternoon, past the heat of the day, when the plants are drier. Make sure the tool is clean and you have fresh "string" reeled out several inches. Wear socks, long pants, and eye protection.

❏ *Check when completed*

❧ TIP 145 ❧

Some plants might be tuckered out
by now. Yank out scraggly annuals,
and cut back flagging perennials.
Assuming the plants are not
diseased or harboring pests, you can
throw all these prunings onto the
compost pile—this way, they'll
contribute to the garden again, later,
when they've broken down.

☐ *Check when completed*

❧ TIP 146 ❧

If a weed problem has gotten out of
hand and you are ready to resort to
herbicides (weed killer), do so
with care. Cut back the offending
patch as much as possible.
Then spray on a dry, windless day.
As a precaution, temporarily
protect nearby desirable plants
with plastic or a tarp.

☐ *Check when completed*

❧ TIP 147 ❧

Set out a hummingbird feeder!
Red-dyed sugar water is now con-
sidered unneeded and possibly not
good for the little birds. Better to fill
a red feeder with colorless sugar
water (one part sugar to four parts
water; mix, boil, and cool before
filling). Flowers they like, such as
honeysuckle and trumpet creeper,
will also keep hummers around.

☐ *Check when completed*

❧ Tip 148 ❧

Combat tunneling rodents that
are dining on your garden from below.
They may be mice or voles, using the
passageways made by moles. (Moles
are actually carnivorous and even eat
grubs.) A cat that's a good hunter is
perhaps your best weapon; traps can
work; poisons should be your last
resort. Also, reduce mulch around
plant stems, which rodents nest in.

☐ *Check when completed*

❦ TIP 149 ❦

Get more shrubs from midsummer's "semi-hardwood" cuttings. These root easily and grow into young plants by fall. Dust the base of pencil-thin shoots with rooting powder, then plant in light, organically rich ground. Water gently and often—they should root in four to six weeks. Good candidates: mock orange, buddleia, viburnum, kerria.

☐ *Check when completed*

❧ TIP 150 ❧

Make delicious berry vinegar.
Start with 3 cups of washed, dried
berries (raspberries, blackberries,
even strawberries). Place in a large
ceramic or glass bowl. Heat 4 cups
of plain white vinegar, stir in
$1/2$ cup sugar until dissolved. Pour
over berries, cover, and let sit for
two days before straining into
decorative glass bottles.

❑ *Check when completed*

❖ TIP 151 ❖

The weed wars are far from over. Under no circumstances should you let annual weeds go to seed! This is how they create a population explosion. As for perennial weeds, late summer is when foliage sends energy down into the root system. Thwart all of them by chopping off their heads, yanking them out, or both.

☐ *Check when completed*

❖ TIP 152 ❖

Gardeners are at risk during summer storms that involve lightning. Water is a great conductor of electricity, so get away from the pool, fountain, sprinklers, and hose. Don't stand under an oak or other tall tree, under an arbor, or in a gazebo. Get in the car, or get in the house.

☐ *Check when completed*

❦ TIP 153 ❦

Walk through and double-check
all your plant supports, from tomato
cages to staked hollyhocks. Rampant
growth and full weight may
have caused them to lean or pulled
them down. Reinsert stakes securely
into the ground, replace missing
ties, and add more ties as needed. In
other words, reestablish order.

☐ *Check when completed*

❧ TIP 154 ❧

Flowerbeds looking heat-stressed?
Take a two-pronged approach to
rejuvenation. First, go out in the
morning while it's cool and tidy up,
clipping off spent blooms and
removing bedraggled and excessive
growth. Second, add or renew a
mulch layer at their feet; this helps
retain some soil moisture and
makes the area look neater.

❏ *Check when completed*

❧ TIP 155 ❧

Cut roses for bouquets. Midmorning is ideal because dew has dried but midday heat is not yet depriving the blooms of moisture. Choose buds that are showing color and just beginning to unfurl—these will finish opening indoors, providing you with quite a show. Cut on an angle, underwater if possible, for maximum water uptake.

☐ *Check when completed*

❧ TIP 156 ❧

How do you know when to harvest a melon? When it's big? When its skin is colorful? When you thump it and hear a deep thud? If these methods sound too vague, don't worry. Harvest when the stem slips readily from the fruit. Pick it up—if the vine falls away, you are free to walk away with the melon.

☐ *Check when completed*

❖ TIP 157 ❖

White grubs in your lawn? Now is
the prime time to go after them.
There are a variety of biologic and
insecticidal treatments that will
control or eradicate these annoying
pests. Start by digging up and taking
a few examples down to your local
garden center so that you get the
right product for the right critter. Fall
lawn aeration will kill some grubs.

☐ *Check when completed*

❧ TIP 158 ❧

Pick and dry fragrant herbs—it's one of gardening's most enchanting chores. Pick lush stems whose blossoms have formed but not yet opened, for maximum scent and flavor. Rinse them quickly and completely pat dry. Make bundles and hang them upside-down in a hot, dark spot, such as an attic. This way, they'll dry before they can rot.

❑ *Check when completed*

❦ TIP 159 ❦

The flowers of your summer bulbs may be past their prime, but be patient with the leaves. Let them die down naturally. They are busy sending valuable starches and sugars into the root system, to fuel next year's display. Don't cut off the leaves until they are completely yellow and limp.

❑ *Check when completed*

❧ TIP 160 ❧

Mail-order bulb catalogs are on
hand now, or you can shop via the
Internet. These outlets will afford
you a far broader selection
of interesting and colorful spring-
flowering bulbs than you'd ever
see at a garden center, so feast your
imagination on the enticing
offerings. Order now so you'll get
them in time for fall planting.

❏ *Check when completed*

❧ TIP 161 ❧

Try some new bulbs this year.
If you like tulips, seek out more
offbeat kinds, like fluted "parrot"
ones or ones with fringed petals.
If you like daffodils, look for the
pink-cupped ones or smaller
flowered but highly fragrant white
ones. Other offbeat bulbs: fritil-
laries, spring snowflake, camassia.

❑ *Check when completed*

❧ TIP 162 ❧

Pick tomatoes! In many varieties, the crop can get so heavy that it pulls down the plant, so you are doing it a favor by removing weight! If you have surplus, give it away, make sauce, or learn how to can. Whatever you do, never refrigerate garden tomatoes—the flesh loses its softness and sweetness.

❑ *Check when completed*

❧ TIP 163 ❧

A whitefly problem can develop if you have potted plants in a warm corner of the porch or deck. One wave of your hand will send up a cloud of these foliage-sucking beasties. Fight back with sprays from the hose. Segregate affected plants, so you can treat them individually and also to improve air circulation.

☐ *Check when completed*

❧ TIP 164 ❧

Support big, floppy perennials
now blooming or about to bloom,
including boltonia, aster, artemisia,
and Japanese anemones. One
effective method is to rig stakes
around the base and run string
between them—a little makeshift
containment fence. Or run string
around a big plant and cinch the
ends to a nearby fence or post.

☐ *Check when completed*

❖ TIP 165 ❖

Extra water is critical in the dog days of August when there is often less rain. Water deeply and regularly at the bases of the plants, where possible. While it can be wasteful, overhead sprinkler watering does help reduce heat stress by lowering leaf temperatures. In any event, water in the morning or evening to avoid moisture evaporation.

❏ *Check when completed*

❧ TIP 166 ❧

Time to pick your glads! Make your
move when the first few buds at the
bottom of the spike are completely
open but the rest are still in bud.
(Leave foliage on the plant; it
replenishes the corm for next year's
show.) Recut the stems indoors, and
put in a vase of lukewarm water;
change the water daily.

❑ *Check when completed*

✤ TIP 167 ✤

Favorite annuals (cleome, cosmos)
going to seed? If you like them,
let them, and you'll have a crowd
next year. But a couple should
be reined in, before it's too late, by
clipping off their fading flowers
or developing seedheads: four 'clocks
(self-sown ones never seem to have
the same pretty colors) and foxgloves
(poisonous to animals).

❑ *Check when completed*

AUGUST

❧ TIP 168 ❧

Do not fertilize your rosebushes
any more, or they'll have reduced
winter hardiness. Also, late doses
inspire a burst of soft green growth
that will be vulnerable to frost.
Enjoy the remaining buds and
blossoms—in the garden or in
bouquets. The bushes will continue
to be productive for a while yet.

❑ *Check when completed*

❦ TIP 169 ❦

Fruit trees ought to be bearing
about this time. Wait till the
color is good before picking. If you
miss the boat and ripe fruit
falls on the ground, snag it right
away. It may be just fine. If you
leave it there, it's only going to rot,
attracting bees and disease.

❑ *Check when completed*

❖ TIP 170 ❖

Dried flowers for arrangements
and craft projects are easy to
make. Just remember that whatever
form or stage the blooms are in,
that's how they'll dry, with no
changes. Array them on screens in a
hot, dry, well-ventilated room. Or
place them in plastic boxes of silica
gel for a few days.

❏ *Check when completed*

❧ TIP 171 ❧

Install a new brick or flagstone
path—a much easier job in dry
weather. Carve out the course with
a shovel to a depth of several inches,
then fill with a base of sand or sand
dust. Wiggle the bricks or stones
into place, separating them by an
inch or less. Water down, let settle,
add more sand if needed.

☐ *Check when completed*

❧ TIP 172 ❧

Cut fragrant flowers early in the day
while they are full of moisture.
Scent resides within the cells
of the petals, so the higher the
water content, the higher
the amount of scent ingredient.
Prolong the delight by displaying
them in a vase that is set in
indirect or low light.

❑ *Check when completed*

❧ TIP 173 ❧

Harvest your cucumbers, squash,
and zucchini on an almost daily
basis. This practice encourages more
production; plus you don't
want them to rot on the vine.
Donate your surplus to a local food
bank (they usually get canned
goods—homegrown produce
will be a treat).

❑ *Check when completed*

❧ TIP 174 ❧

Now is a fine time to attend to your
bearded iris plants. Pry up the
clump with a garden fork.
Cut the foliage low; then split it into
clumps, each with some fat
rhizomes and a little fan of leaves.
Replant and water—there's time for
the divisions to get established
before cold weather arrives.

☐ *Check when completed*

❧ TIP 175 ❧

Watch your potato plants, and once
you see the foliage dying down, dig
down and pull up your harvest.
Wipe the spuds with a damp cloth,
let them dry, and store them in the
refrigerator until you are ready to
cook. Leave the ones you don't need
yet in the ground, though; they'll
keep better there, for now.

☐ *Check when completed*

❧ TIP 176 ❧

Shop the sales at the garden center!
Perennials, ornamental grasses,
even rosebushes may be offered
at bargain prices. If it's still too hot
to plant, hold these in their pots in a
sheltered location for a couple of
weeks. Just remember to stop by
often, even daily, to see whether
they need a drink of water.

❏ *Check when completed*

❧ TIP 177 ❧

Some annuals, having exhausted
themselves and unable to continue
in the summer heat, will quit
blooming around now. They are not
going to magically revive later.
The show is over; yank them out.
Toss them on the compost pile.
Meanwhile, back in the garden,
either replace them with fresh rein-
forcements or mulch over the gap.

☐ *Check when completed*

❧ TIP 178 ❧

Cut your dahlias as often as you can. The more you harvest, the more the plants will produce—you can't say that about every flower, but dahlias never disappoint. Just be sure you have a tall and sturdy vase (something tilt-proof!) to hold them, because some varieties are quite big and top-heavy.

❏ *Check when completed*

❧ TIP 179 ❧

Cease and desist fertilizing your flowerbeds. Most plants are past their prime anyway, flowering finished or almost finished, so there is no benefit. The food would only get the plants to generate fresh new growth—which you don't want to sprout just as cooler weather is starting to arrive.

☐ *Check when completed*

❧ TIP 180 ❧

Keep an eye on your lawn and be ready to mow again as needed. Lawn grass slows growth in hot spells and resumes when the weather cools down. Meanwhile, don't deprive it of water—but don't overdo either. Deliver about an inch of water every few days, or whenever the grass looks wilted.

❑ *Check when completed*

❧ Fall ❧

❧ EVERYDAY TIP ❧

Visit a public garden, or go on a
garden tour. Bring your camera and,
just as important, a notebook.
With or without the help of a guide,
you will find plenty to learn and lots
of inspiration. Be sure to write
down the names of plants or plant
combinations you admire (if there
are no labels, ask someone).

❦ TIP 181 ❦

Find out your area's predicted
first fall frost date. Check your local
paper, or call a garden center or
nearby Cooperative Extension
office. Though it's usually not till
later this month or October,
depending on where you live, you
need to know now so you can
calculate how much gardening
time you have left.

❏ *Check when completed*

❧ TIP 182 ❧

Time to tuck in some color in the garden gaps! Nurseries and garden centers will have plenty of sedums and ornamental kales and cabbages for sale. These are favorites, with good reason. They're durable and long-lasting, and as temperatures drop, their color often gets richer. Mums are also offered in a rainbow of hues—mix and match!

❏ *Check when completed*

❧ TIP 183 ❧

Plant garlic four to six weeks before the ground freezes. Fertile soil is important, but even more important is well drained soil, lest your bulbs rot in soggy ground. (Growing garlic in a raised bed works great.) Plant individual cloves an inch deep, pointed end up, and mulch well. Most aboveground growth won't occur till spring.

❑ *Check when completed*

❧ TIP 184 ❧

Hot days and cool nights can cause
tomatoes to develop unsightly splits
in the sides of the fruit. If you are
worried this is going to happen, try
to moderate the effects by keeping
the plants evenly moist. Also,
don't leave fruits on the vine too
long—harvest them as soon as you
see early signs of marring.

❏ *Check when completed*

❧ TIP 185 ❧

Are your daylilies overcrowded and
blooming sparsely? Divide them
now to jumpstart your spring display.
Prepare the new bed or area first,
though, so the roots won't dry out.
Dig up the clumps, and divide
into sections (back-to-back gardening
forks might be needed). Replant
pieces that include a good chunk of
roots and topgrowth.

❏ *Check when completed*

❧ TIP 186 ❧

Autumn is a fine time to lay turfgrass sod, especially suitable for slopes. Remove rocks, weeds, and roots. Till lightly to loosen the soil, sprinkle a little slow-acting lawn fertilizer (follow directions on the bag), and rake smooth. Put the sod down on a cool, cloudy day, and water well. Keeping seams and edges moist is critical!

❑ *Check when completed*

❧ TIP 187 ❧

Now is also a good time to sow cool-season lawn grass seed mix. Clear out the planting area, add weed-free organic matter, and rake smooth. If you don't use a mechanical seeder, just broadcast left to right, and then up and down, to make sure the whole area is covered. Keep constantly moist so the seeds can germinate and seedlings develop a strong root system.

☐ *Check when completed*

❧ TIP 188 ❧

Do you feel like your autumn
landscape lacks color and punch?
Visit some public or private gardens
find out what is looking fabulous
right now in your area. Perhaps you
can plant something this year;
if not, make a wish list and act on it
next spring. Check out the
many types of asters now available!

❑ *Check when completed*

❧ TIP 189 ❧

Plant a shrub or tree. The soil is still warm, and drenching fall rains will help water it in. Dig an ample hole. Mix native soil with some organic matter for backfilling only if the soil is heavily clay. Set the plant at or above the level it was growing in the pot, and press the dirt firmly around it. Water weekly until the ground freezes.

☐ *Check when completed*

❧ TIP 190 ❧

Harvest and cure onions.
While they're still in the ground,
knock over their tops with a
rake. Make your move a week
later—get them out of the ground,
wipe them free of dirt, and
arrange on screens to dry. Only
then can you clip off their tops.
Store in a cool, dry place.

❑ *Check when completed*

❖ TIP 191 ❖

Deciduous trees that bleed sap after spring pruning—notably birches and maples—can be trimmed now with little risk. Use the same system; that is, take out all "non-negotiable" growth first, such as dead and damaged wood. Then thin, including taking out crossing branches. Finally, shorten good limbs by a few inches all around as you shape.

☐ *Check when completed*

❧ TIP 192 ❧

Make a colorful fall arrangement.
Start with a few branches of
vivid fall foliage. Fill in with softer
textured but bright fall perennials
such as goldenrod and purple
asters. Add a few branches that are
adorned with red berries or red
rose hips (strip foliage from these).
Use the seedheads of ornamental
grasses as dramatic filler.

❑ *Check when completed*

SEPTEMBER

❧ TIP 193 ❧

Feed your trees and shrubs one last
time. At this point in the year, shoot
growth has ceased and the still
actively growing roots of woody
plants will make most efficient use
of the fertilizer's nutrients.
Research has shown that early
spring growth depends heavily on
this stored bounty.

❏ *Check when completed*

❧ TIP 194 ❧

Fertilize the lawn. It's much
smarter to do this now, rather than
in the spring (when the food
would also inspire a fresh growth
spurt from weeds!). Topgrowth is
slowing down or finished, so the
nutrients will fortify the roots.
Remember to water before and after
for the best uptake.

❏ *Check when completed*

❧ TIP 195 ❧

Dig up gladiolus corms and
dahlia tubers. Get them out of the
ground before it freezes, dry them
on screens for a day or two, and
then clean them off. Store them
in bags in a frost-free spot. Don't
forget to label! And sprinkle a
little fungicide dust into each
bag to prevent rot.

❏ *Check when completed*

❧ TIP 196 ❧

Bring some tender herbs in for the winter. Cut them back to live growth first. Then dig them up and put them in pots, watering well. Leave the pots in a sheltered area for a while, checking on them from time to time, just to get them used to container life. Move them indoors when frost threatens.

❑ *Check when completed*

❧ TIP 197 ❧

Plant some peonies! These
beautiful, tough perennials relish
an organically rich soil. The only
tricky part is placing them at the
proper planting depth—the little
pink "eyes" (buds) on their clumping
roots should end up no more than
2 inches below the soil surface.

❑ *Check when completed*

❧ TIP 198 ❧

Buy some bales of straw or
hay to stockpile for winter
mulching. Straw has fewer weed
seeds than regular hay. Best of all is
salt-marsh hay, if you can get it. It's
mainly dried sea grasses, and if there
are seeds present, they won't
germinate in your garden because
they need salty conditions.

❑ *Check when completed*

❧ TIP 199 ❧

Start raking fall leaves. If you wait
till they all drop, the job can be too
big! Scoot piles off to one side or
stuff them in paper bags as you
work. You can compost them or use
them as a mulch (chopped up,
preferably—run over them with
the lawn mower).

❑ *Check when completed*

❧ TIP 200 ❧

Have you admired those
random but bright and colorful
drifts of spring bulbs, but wondered
how to get that spontaneous
"naturalized" look? It's easy. Just toss
handfuls into the chosen area and
plant each one where it lands. Dig a
hole twice as deep as the bulb's size,
sprinkle in some compost, set in the
bulb, cover, and water.

❏ *Check when completed*

❧ TIP 201 ❧

Continue to mow the lawn over
2 inches tall as long as it is
growing to keep it looking neat.
This sends it into winter looking
as good as can be expected and
means it will be in better shape next
spring when growth ramps up
again. Mow the final leaf drop and
leave it to topdress the turf.

☐ *Check when completed*

❧ TIP 202 ❧

Buying bulbs locally? Examine each one. It should be clean, with no blemishes. Squeeze it to be sure it is firm and plump. Compare it to its fellows and choose the heftier ones (light ones are dried up inside). Note that comparatively bigger ones have more stored reserves and thus are more likely to put on a big show.

❑ *Check when completed*

SEPTEMBER

❧ TIP 203 ❧

Lay out and prepare a new bed.
You may have more time,
energy, and enthusiasm for this
project now than in the spring.
Mark the boundaries, dig out
obstructions, and mix in plenty of
organic matter to a depth of several
inches. Then cover with black
plastic or mulch and let it all meld
over the winter months.

❏ *Check when completed*

❧ TIP 204 ❧

Clean up your roses! Don't
prune—but it's okay to remove
spent flowers and dead or damaged
stems and leaves. Be sure to clean up
under the plants, too, as pests and
diseases can lay dormant in debris
that is left behind. Last but not
least, water well.

❏ *Check when completed*

❖ TIP 205 ❖

Devote a few hours to planting
tulips. Select a sunny spot with well-
drained soil—soggy ground is
fatal. Plant them a safe distance
down, 6 to 8 inches or so, to avoid
any chance of frost-heaving.
Give them good sandy loam, a dash
of compost, and a good watering
when you're done. (Deer love tulips;
protect them next spring.)

❑ *Check when completed*

❧ TIP 206 ❧

Fertilize existing and new bulb plantings with care. Use slow-acting plant food in the bed so it does not burn tender roots at a time when they don't need any stress. Alternately, "top-dress" bulbs by sprinkling granular fertilizer on the surface and watering it in. Holland Bulb Booster™ (9-9-6) is great for tulips and members of the lily family.

❑ *Check when completed*

❧ TIP 207 ❧

Wrap large tub-grown shrubs or
trees for the winter. The easiest,
most effective way to do this
is to create a column of chicken wire
all around the pot and twice as
tall, at least. Dump in fall leaves.
Add a cover, or encase the entire
thing in hardware cloth or burlap.

❑ *Check when completed*

❦ TIP 208 ❦

Time to start bringing tender
and tropical potted plants
inside. Give them one last good
watering outside, and check
thoroughly for insect pests. Cut off
all remaining flower stalks and
scraggly foliage. Find them a cool,
nonfreezing spot, such as an
enclosed porch or sunroom.

❏ *Check when completed*

❧ TIP 209 ❧

Foil rodents that like to eat your tulip bulbs. "Cage" the bulbs, making a box out of chicken wire that you fill with soil and bulbs. The roots will be able grow through the bottom, and in spring, the foliage and stalks will make it to the light.

❑ *Check when completed*

❧ TIP 210 ❧

Watch for bugs that try to enter your home or garage looking for shelter and warmth. Common culprits include ladybugs, or box elder beetles. They won't harm wood, pets, or you, but they are a nuisance. Your best bet is to thwart them with caulking and weather-stripping.

❏ *Check when completed*

❖ TIP 211 ❖

Cut back your taller perennials before frost comes—even if there's some lingering live growth, flowers, or seedheads. Chopping down to within a few inches above the soil level seems brutal, but it will do no harm and the way will be cleared for next spring's resurgence.

❑ *Check when completed*

❖ TIP 212 ❖

Spare a few perennials whose dried flowers have winter value. Birds may enjoy the dried flowerheads, either as a place to alight or as a seed source. And whenever snow finally arrives, some of these plants look beautiful with a jaunty white cap. Examples include ornamental grasses, echinacea, rudbeckia, sedum, and astilbe.

☐ *Check when completed*

❧ TIP 213

Time to close down the vegetable
garden. Pull out and compost
all plant debris, with the exception
of anything that was diseased
(bag up that stuff and send it away
with the household trash). Mulch
with chopped-up fall leaves or
compost (or both), which you can
dig in next spring.

❏ *Check when completed*

❧ TIP 214 ❧

Get ready for an indoor holiday
forced bulb display now—most take
six to ten weeks to bloom. Pot up
tulips, hyacinths, grape hyacinths,
and daffodils. Use a light, sterile
potting mix and plant more shallowly
than you would outside, around 1 or
2 inches deep. Label, water, and set
them in a dark, cool place for the
necessary chilling period.

❑ *Check when completed*

❧ TIP 215 ❧

Send your broadleaf evergreens
into winter in good shape. Water
each one deeply one last time before
the ground freezes. Once it does,
spray the entire foliage with an
"antidesiccant" (available at a garden
center—follow the directions on the
label). This keeps the leaves from
curling and drying (winter, actually,
is a time of drought).

❑ *Check when completed*

OCTOBER

✤ TIP 216 ✤

Shield your evergreens, if
they are marginally hardy or
growing in an exposed or windy
location. Some people make
plywood tents, which is fine, if the
wood is not flimsy and you can
make them secure. Otherwise, a
cage of burlap supported by
wooden stakes also does the trick.
Do not cover with plastic.

☐ *Check when completed*

OCTOBER

❖ TIP 217 ❖

Protect your ripening pumpkins.
About now, the skin should be hard
and the color should be darkening,
but if they are exposed to a frost,
they will turn black—what a disap-
pointment. Just cover the plant with
a tarp for the night if the forecast is
for subfreezing temperatures.

❑ *Check when completed*

❧ TIP 218 ❧

Plant a balled-and-burlapped
evergreen. Set it into a hole that
is about the same depth as the
rootball but three times wider—
the roots like to spread outward.
Mix good organic matter (compost
or dampened peat moss) with the
native soil (if the soil is poor) when
backfilling. Handle the plant by the
rootball as you work. Water well.

☐ *Check when completed*

❧ TIP 219 ❧

Pick the last tomatoes, especially if frost threatens. Help partially ripe ones continue to turn red by placing them in a bowl with an apple. The ethylene gas that a ripe apple naturally emits hastens this process (no, it's not that the apple is "showing them how it's done"!).

❏ *Check when completed*

❧ TIP 220 ❧

Harvest sunflower seeds—assuming
the birds haven't beaten you
to it. Cut the flowerhead off with
about a foot of stem attached and
hang it in a dry, airy location to
finish ripening. Whatever you do,
don't stack or bag the heads, or they
will rot. Ripe seeds can be flicked
off and dried further.

❑ *Check when completed*

❧ TIP 221 ❧

When the mums start to fade, don't treat them like expensive annuals. They are easy to winter over. Just dig them up, rootball and all, and transfer them to a cold frame. Cover with mulch. Alternatively, leave them where they are growing but mulch heavily. Being subjected to freeze-thaw cycles is what kills them.

❏ *Check when completed*

❧ TIP 222 ❧

Rescue your tuberous begonias.
Frost will kill them, so act today.
Dig them up or knock them out of
their pots. Clip off topgrowth;
yanking it exposes the tubers to rot.
Shake off the soil, let them dry out
for a week or so, then store in a bag
of dry vermiculite in a cool spot (the
fridge will do, if you have room).

❏ *Check when completed*

❖ TIP 223 ❖

Parsley can be saved. You may already have noticed it is a cold-tolerant herb. Pick the last green stems, rinse off the dirt, and dry with paper towels. Place them into a plastic baggie, squeeze the air out, and seal. The contents will keep in the freezer for months.

❏ *Check when completed*

❖ TIP 224 ❖

Buy birdseed. The widely
available mixes are not always the
best bet, though. These tend to
attract undesirable birds and pesky
rodents (such as squirrels, raccoons,
and rats). Instead, look for
100 percent sunflower seed, nyjer
seed (thistle), or safflower seed—
nutritious treats favored by smaller
migrating songbirds.

❏ *Check when completed*

❧ TIP 225 ❧

Renew the organic matter
in the tidied-up vegetable garden
and now-emptied flowerbeds.
Do this before the ground freezes.
Well-rotted compost is ideal, or
you can buy bagged compost.
Dehydrated cow manure and
chopped-up fall leaves are also good.
Dig and mix everything to a depth
of 6 or more inches.

❑ *Check when completed*

❖ TIP 226 ❖

Sow a cover crop in any open spot in need of organic matter. These annuals germinate in cooler, moist soil and may even grow some on milder days. You'll till them under next spring. They will stop erosion and prevent nutrients from leaching away over the winter months. (What kind? Get advice from your local garden center or Extension agent.)

❏ *Check when completed*

❖ TIP 227 ❖

Bring along a shovel and "edit" your garden—this is an ideal time to remove plants that didn't work out. Perhaps they took up too much space or didn't perform well, or maybe you simply didn't end up liking the way they look. Dig them up and give them away or toss their remains on the compost pile.

❑ *Check when completed*

❧ TIP 228 ❧

Remove root suckers from your apple and crabapple trees—suckers both divert energy from the tree and detract from its appearance. Gently digging down to the source of the sucker, with your fingers or a trowel, will provide more complete removal than just lopping it off.

❑ *Check when completed*

❧ TIP 229 ❧

Protect marginally hardy rosebushes. Grafted ones, in particular,
have a hard time in cold winters,
often dying down to the rootstock
(thus the roses you wanted are
killed off). Shovel lots of
mulch over the base of the plant, up
and over the bulging graft. Or
place a cage over the entire plant
and fill with mulch.

❑ *Check when completed*

❧ TIP 230 ❧

Protect a marginally hardy
climbing rose for the winter. Wear
tough gloves and protective clothing
if it's a thorny one. Get up on a
ladder and carefully remove the
canes from the support or trellis.
Lower them onto the ground, peg
them in place, and cover with
plenty of mulch.

❑ *Check when completed*

❧ TIP 231 ❧

Shorter days with less light inspire
spider plants to form "spiders" at
last. Let these grow to several
inches big, then sever them from
the mother plant and pot up.
Nurture them in a warm, bright
room for now; don't neglect
watering. Later, you can move
them into their own hanging
basket or give them away.

☐ *Check when completed*

❧ TIP 232 ❧

Protect garden concrete and terra-cotta—such as pots, urns, statuary, and birdbaths—from winter damage. Because it absorbs water that can freeze, concrete cracks all too easily. Bring indoors or waterproof them with a silicon-based water seal, a paint meant for outdoor use, or even a thin layer of white cement. At least, cover or turn over vulnerable pieces.

❏ *Check when completed*

❧ TIP 233 ❧

Save the seeds that you scoop out of
your Halloween jack-o-lantern.
Spread them out and dry them on a
tray or paper plate, then put
them out for the birds. A platform
bird feeder displays and holds
them well. Cardinals in particular
relish this treat.

❏ *Check when completed*

❧ TIP 234 ❧

If you haven't already done so,
cover the grill and your lawn
furniture for the winter. Or bring
them into a protected area inside,
such as the garage or basement. If
you leave these things exposed to
the elements for many months,
no matter how durable they are,
there's likely to be damage or fading.

❑ *Check when completed*

❧ TIP 235 ❧

Clean your outdoor cushions. Use a
stiff brush to get off dirt; then
whack out the dust. Put them to dry
in a warm area for several days, such
as the laundry room (better still, if
they will fit, run them through the
dryer). There must be absolutely no
lingering moisture, or they will
mildew or become smelly in storage.

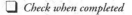 *Check when completed*

❧ TIP 236 ❧

Drain the hose and bring it
in for the winter. Wipe down its
surface with a cloth so there's
no moisture or mud. Don't hang it.
Store it flat, someplace dry
and dark. Let it coil the way it does
naturally; forcing it in other
ways, especially when it is cold,
leads to cracks.

❏ *Check when completed*

❖ TIP 237 ❖

Close up the compost pile for the
winter. Its activity has been slowing
for a while now, and tossing kitchen
scraps on it at this point leads
only to a pile of chilly or frozen
garbage that doesn't break down.
Give it one last stir, if possible;
then replace the lid or cover it with
a tarp to discourage rodents.

❑ *Check when completed*

❧ TIP 238 ❧

Prevent small, fragile conifers from winter damage. Winter ice and snow can snap or bend their branches, harming their health and marring their compact look. Just take a long strip of fabric, about 2 inches wide, and wind it around the plant from the bottom to the top, securing the branches.

❏ *Check when completed*

❧ TIP 239 ❧

Prevent the possibility of snow mold
forming on your lawn over the
winter months. Thoroughly rake
any fall leaves that have not been
chopped by the mower to be
topdressing. Then, if feasible, mow
the lawn one last time at about
2 inches high, because this fungal
disease breeds in taller lawn grass.

❏ *Check when completed*

❧ TIP 240 ❧

Check on your pots of forced bulbs. They should be in a cool but not freezing area. If they're in the path of foot traffic (the basement stairs, for instance), try to find a safer spot. Keep their soil moistened but by no means soggy, and watch for signs of sprouts.

❑ *Check when completed*

❧ TIP 241 ❧

You may still be able to harvest some cold-weather crops out of the vegetable garden. Root crops in particular do okay. Indeed, turnips seem to be even sweeter if the weather is cold and the ground chilly. Just push aside protective mulch and haul out what you need.

❏ *Check when completed*

❖ TIP 242 ❖

If you have a black walnut tree, this is the time of year you are glad of it (its inhibiting effect on plants grown near it is well documented). However, those tasty nuts are encased in a stubborn husk. If hitting them with a hammer doesn't work, lay the nuts on the driveway and drive the car over them.

❑ *Check when completed*

❧ TIP 243 ❧

Are some of your fall-planted bulbs peeking up right now? Grape hyacinths and Madonna lilies will do this some years, especially if winter is arriving slowly. Don't be alarmed; they aren't actually poised to flower too soon. Throw a little extra mulch over them if you want.

❏ *Check when completed*

❧ TIP 244 ❧

Empty all the windowboxes,
now, when you finally have time.
Discard the soil mix, as well
as the dead plants. Scrub them out a
bit with a brush, and wipe them
down inside and out. It doesn't take
long, and you'll be glad you did
this when spring returns and you get
in the mood to refill them.

❑ *Check when completed*

❧ TIP 245 ❧

Move emptied pots and containers of all kinds out of the weather. Rinse them out if they're dirty, and stack them in the garage, shed, or basement. Instead of getting rid of cracked clay pots, break them into small pieces and save these; they may come in handy for a drainage layer another day.

❑ *Check when completed*

NOVEMBER

❖ TIP 246 ❖

Take the day to sit down and
update your garden log or journal.
Do this now before you get too busy
with holiday preparations—and
while the garden you recently
enjoyed is still fresh in your
memory. Make notes and resolu-
tions for next year's garden.

❑ *Check when completed*

❧ TIP 247 ❧

Buy amaryllis bulbs right now, if
you want them to be part of your
late-winter or holiday season décor.
They typically take six to eight
weeks to bloom. Get prepotted
"kits," or buy loose bulbs and pot
them yourself. Just remember that
the hefty bulb should be set
half-in, half-out of the mix.

❏ *Check when completed*

❧ TIP 248 ❧

Harvest those vegetables that
tolerate a frost: broccoli, brussels
sprouts, cauliflower, cabbage, and
the like. Clean them well before
eating them raw or cooking them.
They might inspire you to
make a hot homemade soup. Extras
will keep well in a cool, dark
place or the fridge.

☐ *Check when completed*

NOVEMBER

❧ TIP 249 ❧

Deal with overhanging or otherwise
risky tree branches now, before
winter comes and a burden of snow
or ice causes them to fall. Call a
tree service, get a written estimate,
ask if they are insured, and
supervise the removal. If you want
the wood for firewood or another
use, speak up.

☐ *Check when completed*

❧ TIP 250 ❧

Planning to buy a living Christmas
tree this year, and plant it in the
yard after the holidays? Don't buy it
yet—but it would be smart
to decide where its permanent
outdoor home will be . . . and
to dig the hole now, before the
ground is frozen solid. That way,
you'll be ready to go.

❑ *Check when completed*

❧ TIP 251 ❧

Rake up the last of the fall leaves.
Don't put them directly on
flowerbeds or the vegetable garden
(even though it's tempting).
They'll only mat down. Run them
through a shredder, or pass over
them with the lawnmower; then
consolidate them in their own pile
(not the compost pile). You'll be able
to use them next year.

❑ *Check when completed*

❦ TIP 252 ❦

Mist your indoor plants.
When the heat comes on in the
house this time of year, the air
quickly gets dry. Your houseplants
may suffer from this sudden
lack of humidity, and spritzing
them with water will help them. (If
you don't have a good mister, why
not go out and buy one?)

❑ *Check when completed*

❧ TIP 253 ❧

Stratify seeds that need it—some perennials, some wildflowers. They actually won't germinate unless they get a month or two of winter cold and moisture. Supply this by sowing them into a garden bed now or into flats that you keep outside. Which seeds require stratification? The seed packet will tell you, and tell you for how long.

❑ *Check when completed*

❧ TIP 254 ❧

Protect the young trees in your yard from small rodents, rabbits, and deer that nibble during the winter. If they "girdle" the tree (strip away or destroy bark either part or all the way around), it can die. Thwart these pests by putting a cylinder of hardware cloth around each tree and pressing it into the ground a few inches.

❏ *Check when completed*

❧ TIP 255 ❧

Protect the young trees in your yard from winter "sunscald," literally a sunburn that occurs on the sunny side of the tree during the winter when it is more exposed. Paint the lowest foot or so of the trunk with white latex paint, or install a temporary bandage of burlap.

❑ *Check when completed*

❖ TIP 256 ❖

Make some durable plant labels,
while you have time and are
thinking of it. Then just stash them
away until next spring. You won't
get everything taken care of, of
course, but you can certainly do
ones for major, favorite plants. Write
on metal markers with a grease
pencil or on smooth rocks with a
permanent marker.

❏ *Check when completed*

⚜ TIP 257 ⚜

Browse the gardening section
in your favorite bookstore. New
gardening books are often issued
this time of year, just before the
holiday season. If you don't buy a
title for yourself, at least you can
make a "wish list" and place hints
for friends and relatives.

☐ *Check when completed*

❖ TIP 258 ❖

Move your African violet plants!
Winter's shorter days deprive them
of the 12 to 16 hours of sun that
they prefer each day. You can put
them on a windowsill that faces
either south or east, or be sure to
place them under fluorescent lights.

☐ *Check when completed*

NOVEMBER

❧ TIP 259 ❧

Evaluate your entire houseplant
collection. Pinch off and
discard scraggly growth and spent
flower stalks. Check for lingering
insect pests. In most cases, it is a
good practice to stop fertilizing and
to reduce water for foliage plants for
the winter months so they can have
a rest. Flowering plants need some
fertilizer and regular watering.

☐ *Check when completed*

NOVEMBER

❧ TIP 260 ❧

Attend a winter gardening class or
an interesting lecture. Flyers for
these will be at garden centers, listed
in local newspapers, or described
in the newsletters of nearby botanic
gardens or arboreta. It's good to get
out of the house—and always
worthwhile to get educated and
inspired in the off-season.

❏ *Check when completed*

❧ TIP 261 ❧

Evaluate your vegetable garden and make notes for next year. Tuck these notes where you can refer to them early next spring. Do you need more space for ramblers like squash, zucchini, and pumpkin? Did you have too many tomato plants and not enough peppers? Should the entire garden be bigger or smaller?

❑ *Check when completed*

❧ TIP 262 ❧

Shop for the gardeners on your gift list by mail-order catalog (or go to a company's website). Order now so everything arrives in time and you avoid last-minute rush-shipping fees. If you can't decide—or you want to give a plant of their own choosing—get a gift certificate or a membership to a local arboretum.

❑ *Check when completed*

❧ TIP 263 ❧

Stop in at the local garden center
now and buy lots of paper-white
narcissus bulbs for forcing—they
may be cheaper when purchased in
large quantities. Keep some for
yourself, and save the spares for gift-
giving. (You can also give the
recipient a suitable pot and some
pebbles; if this is your plan,
get all the supplies now.)

❑ *Check when completed*

❧ TIP 264 ❧

Did you know there's an annual that is not an annual, one you can easily overwinter? It's your potted geranium (really a pelargonium). Cut it back to a few inches high, thus removing most or all of its leaves and stems, and place it in a cool room. Keep its soil mix lightly moist all winter, and it will revive next spring.

❑ *Check when completed*

❖ TIP 265 ❖

Create a Thanksgiving centerpiece
for the dinner or buffet table. Cut
sprigs from evergreens in the yard
and supplement these with some
store-bought flowers. Orchids,
carnations, and roses are abundant
at the florist this time of year and go
well. Keep the arrangement fresh by
holding it in the fridge or a cold
room until you set the table.

❏ *Check when completed*

❧ TIP 266 ❧

Assuming the ground is now
frozen, protect precious or
marginally hardy woodland ground-
covers. Scatter a foot-deep layer
of hay over the area, fluffing it up as
you work (to maximize air space).
This will trap heat radiating up
from the ground; eventually snow
will pack it down. Both ways,
it is a fine insulator.

❏ *Check when completed*

❧ TIP 267 ❧

Dreaming of a conservatory, a potting shed, or other major garden-ing structure? The off-season is the ideal time to do some research, finding out what is available and what you can afford. Scan gardening magazines for ads or surf the Internet, and send away for promo-tional material. Note that some models are "you-assemble kits."

☐ *Check when completed*

❧ TIP 268 ❧

Order gardening catalogs; get "on the list" now, before they mail. If you received one last year, and especially if you ordered from a company last year, chances are you'll get another. For all others, fill out the form provided on the website or send a postcard request. If they charge a small fee, be sure to send a check.

❑ *Check when completed*

❧ TIP 269 ❧

Did a persistent pest or disease
problem in the garden trouble you
this past year? Try to learn more
about it—what causes or attracts it,
and which plants are favored or
targeted. Review the strategies
you've already tried. Draw up a
battle plan for next year.

❑ *Check when completed*

❧ TIP 270 ❧

Mulch the garlic you planted
in the fall, if you haven't already
done so. Because the bulbs are not
planted deeply, they are vulnerable
to frost heaving and frigid soil
conditions. So a good, thick layer of
organic mulch is in order. Chopped
fall leaves are just fine.

❑ *Check when completed*

❧ WINTER ❧

❧ EVERYDAY TIP ❧

You don't have to be a Latin
scholar, but it helps to learn the
basics of the scientific plant
naming system. The first word
(italic and always capitalized) is the
genus, and the second word
is the species. If there is another
word set off by single quotation
marks, then that is a specific variety
sometimes called a cultivar.

❧ TIP 271 ❧

Clean off caked-on dirt and mud from shovels and other large implements before putting them away for the winter. Fill a bucket with sand and mix in some vegetable oil until it's moistened. Plunge in the blade of each dirty tool. The sand's abrasion will help clean it off and the oil will coat the tool, which prevents rust.

☐ *Check when completed*

❧ TIP 272 ❧

Check on pots of forced bulbs,
which you stored in a dark, cool
spot and have been moistening from
time to time. If they have finally
sprouted and are showing flower
stalks or buds, it's time to bring
them into a bright, warm room.
Here, you can look after them as
they grow faster. Soon they'll burst
into glorious bloom.

❏ *Check when completed*

❧ TIP 273 ❧

Is there a spot you neglected to
mulch? Even if the ground is
frozen or snow has fallen, it's not
too late. Scoop on the mulch
anyway! Its natural warmth will
melt any snow and it will settle
into place and buffer soil
temperature over the plants or
area you want to protect.

❑ *Check when completed*

❧ TIP 274 ❧

Save fireplace ashes, assuming you burn regular hardwood logs, not anything with additives. Just scoop them into a bag or bucket and reserve them in a dry place. These can be used in the spring as a soil amendment. They offer potash and lime for your plants if a soil test indicates this is needed.

❑ *Check when completed*

❧ TIP 275 ❧

Decorate empty windowboxes and planter boxes. Fill them with ever-green cuttings, holly sprigs, even dried seedheads of ornamental grasses. The colder air this time of year should keep them looking intact for at least a few weeks. To keep this material from falling over or blowing away, anchor it with a hidden brick or two, or some rocks.

☐ *Check when completed*

❧ TIP 276 ❧

The best living evergreen trees for indoor as well as outdoor holiday decorating are Alberta spruces. Buy some wherever holiday supplies or plants are sold. They are popular because they have a dense, compact growth habit and tolerate cold weather. Give them occasional light waterings, though; they are alive, after all!

❑ *Check when completed*

❧ TIP 277 ❧

Safely adorn outdoor plants with strands of lights. Work on a day when conditions are not wet or icy. Drape the lights first, before connecting them to an outdoor electrical cord. Work from the top of the plant down. If you use a ladder, seat it securely first and have a helper hold it steady.

❑ *Check when completed*

❖ TIP 278 ❖

Place poinsettia plants wisely, so
they will look good as long as
possible. A windowsill location that
gets six hours of light (but not direct
sunlight) per day is ideal. Avoid
drafty areas and temperatures under
70 degrees Fahrenheit or so. A spot
close to a heat source, however, dries
out the plant and causes the flowers
(actually, colorful bracts) to fade.

❏ *Check when completed*

❧ TIP 279 ❧

Does the flower stalk of your
amaryllis need staking?
Some varieties are short and stout
and don't need support, but
taller ones benefit. Garden retailers
sell special amaryllis stakes that
support those fabulous but top-
heavy flowers. Plunge it
into the soil below a safe distance
from the fat bulb.

❑ *Check when completed*

❖ TIP 280 ❖

Make herb-flavored olive oils
to give as holiday gifts. Buy small
glass containers that seal securely
with a cork or stopper. Wedge in
some sprigs from your overwintered
potted herbs: rosemary, oregano,
thyme, or a combination. Drizzle in
the oil and seal. Affix some pretty
labels, and voilà!

❑ *Check when completed*

❧ TIP 281 ❧

Decorate an outdoor tree to attract hungry overwintering birds. Drape it with garlands made of popcorn, cranberries, peanuts still in their shells, raisins, and bits of orange peel. Hang carrots, apples, colorful Indian corn, and chunks of suet. As the saying goes, "If you build it, they will come"!

❑ *Check when completed*

❧ TIP 282 ❧

Make ornaments from pinecones. Bring them indoors a few days ahead of time, and set them in a warm place. This dries them out completely, evicts lingering bugs, and ensures that they are fully open. Roll them in household glue and dust them with colorful sequins or glitter. Fashion loops from ribbons or yarn.

❑ *Check when completed*

❧ TIP 283 ❧

Bring more pots of sprouting forced bulbs from their cold storage into the house proper. Water them well, and place them in bright but indirect light. To help the flowers last longer, don't display them anywhere close to a heat source, particularly not the mantelpiece.

☐ *Check when completed*

❧ TIP 284 ❧

Expand your selection of cut winter
greens beyond the traditional.
If you have access to these (on your
property or by permission), consider
rhododendron, evergreen magnolia,
yellow- and green-variegated
acuba, and Japanese umbrella pine
branches. Add sprigs of berry-
covered deciduous holly for color.

❑ *Check when completed*

❧ TIP 285 ❧

Make a wreath from evergreen
cuttings in your own yard. Visit a
hobby store and buy a round wire
base, green plastic tape, and green
florist's wire. Press dampened moss
into the base, and wind the tape
around it to hold it in place; make a
wire hook at the top. Poke in the
cuttings thickly all around.

☐ *Check when completed*

❧ TIP 286 ❧

Make evergreen swags for your
holiday décor. Use cuttings from
your yard or the woods; strip their
bases up a few inches. Twist
florist's wire around the ends, and
then attach them along the length of
wire or rope. Enough greens will
hide the wire from view.

❑ *Check when completed*

❖ TIP 287 ❖

Are you leaving some office plants
on their own while you take some
time off? Make sure they'll survive
your absence. Soak them well
one last time. Then group them in a
bright spot with indirect light
only. Loosely drape a large, clear
plastic bag (such as a dry-cleaning
bag) over them like a tent.

❏ *Check when completed*

❖ TIP 288 ❖

If you travel anywhere with
live plants, protect them. Water
them a few hours before you leave.
Just before you head out, encase
them in newspaper and staple the
covering closed (florists use this
method, you may have noticed).
Warm up the car before putting
them in. At your destination, hurry
inside and unwrap them at once.

❏ *Check when completed*

❧ TIP 289 ❧

Live-cut Christmas trees fare best if you recut the base before putting it into a clean stand or bucket of water. Do this immediately after purchase. Various preservatives have been suggested, including a penny, a splash of vodka or bleach, and aspirin. You can try these, but most important is to remember to top off often with fresh water.

❑ *Check when completed*

❦ TIP 290 ❦

When wrapping presents, tuck a
sprig of lavender, rosemary, or
other overwintered herb under the
ribbon. Taking the trimmings
won't do the plant any harm this
time of year. And the recipient
will be enchanted with this
pretty and fragrant reminder of
summer days in your garden.

❏ *Check when completed*

❧ TIP 291 ❧

Make some winter potpourri, to
scent the living room or bathroom,
to give away as gifts, or to bring to a
hostess of a holiday party. Mix
spruce or fir sprigs, berries, rose
hips, small pine or spruce cones,
seedpods, and dried flowers and
petals. Add cinnamon sticks for
fragrance. Display in small bowls.

☐ *Check when completed*

⚜ TIP 292 ⚜

Check potted rosemary plants,
a popular gift plant this time of
year. Because it is technically
an evergreen shrub from the
Mediterranean, it becomes unhappy
in moisture-retentive or soggy
soil. You might have to repot yours
into a mix that has lots of sand or
perlite, to improve drainage.

❑ *Check when completed*

❧ TIP 293 ❧

Living and live-cut Christmas
trees can lose needles and dry out
in the warmth of your home.
Even the strings of lights generate a
small amount of heat that adds
to the stress. So keep the soilball or
trunk evenly moist, and turn
off the lights overnight or
when you are out.

❏ *Check when completed*

❖ TIP 294 ❖

Both living and live-cut evergreen
trees dry out easily in warm
houses. Buy them early so they don't
dry out on the sales lot. Plunge the
freshly recut trunk of a live-cut tree
in water as soon as possible. Keep
them cold, even outdoors, until they
are brought inside. Bring them into
warmth gradually and consider
using an antidessicant spray.

❏ *Check when completed*

DECEMBER

❖ TIP 295 ❖

Make an unusual, fresh-looking,
and colorful holiday-table centerpiece this year. Start with a shallow
tray and one or more colorful
pillar candles. Add a thin layer of
water, then fill with salad greens,
cherry tomatoes, and peppers.

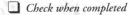

❑ *Check when completed*

DECEMBER

❧ TIP 296 ❧

Take a walk outside. Stay off the
frozen grass, but double-check that
all the coverings and mulches you've
put down are still in place. Carefully
shore up any that have been
displaced. If wind is the culprit, try
covering loose mulch with netting
or wire mesh, anchored with rocks.

❑ *Check when completed*

❧ TIP 297 ❧

Organize your gardening bookshelf,
especially if you receive more titles
as gifts during the holidays.
Separate factual references from
reading-for-pleasure titles. Group
the references by subject or by
season—whatever makes the most
sense to you. Then pick one and put
it on your bedside table!

☐ *Check when completed*

❧ TIP 298 ❧

Retrieve some of your
homegrown onions or potatoes
from storage, and make a hearty
soup. While you are there, take a
few extra moments to check that
none are rotting or sprouting. If
you find damaged or "iffy" produce,
discard it immediately so the
problem doesn't spread.

❏ *Check when completed*

❧ TIP 299 ❧

As soon as you are sure the ground is frozen, gather up some evergreen boughs (left over from the holidays?) and put them over your perennial and bulb beds. This holds insulating mulch and snow in place. You don't want to do this too early, though, or damaging mice and other rodents might move in.

❑ *Check when completed*

DECEMBER

❖ TIP 300 ❖

Since light is low this time of year,
some of your houseplants might be
suffering a bit. If they're developing
lanky stems or yellow leaves,
or if the entire plant is leaning
towards the nearest light source, it's
time to intervene and help. Move
them, even if temporarily, to a
brighter spot—a sunnier, south-
facing window or under lights.

❑ *Check when completed*

❖ TIP 301 ❖

Hang a wall calendar for the
coming year, one with big squares
that you can write gardening notes
and ideas onto. Tack it up at eye
level in a high-traffic spot so you
will refer to it often. (Maybe you
received one with a gardening theme
as a gift—if not, they go on
sale about now!)

❏ *Check when completed*

❧ TIP 302 ❧

After a heavy snowfall, pull on your
boots, go out, and patrol the yard
to ward off potential damage—
such as bent or broken limbs—to
your trees, shrubs, and hedges. Use
a broom, in a downward-sweeping
motion, to clear chunks of snow
from evergreen branches. Wiggle or
shake bent, snow-burdened limbs.

❑ *Check when completed*

❧ Tip 303 ❧

Inventory your seed stash. Some leftovers from last year may still be good, assuming you stored the packets in a dry, cool place. Larger seeds (beans, squash, nasturtium, and morning glory) are more likely to be viable than small seeds (carrots, lettuce, columbines, and poppies). Tiny seeds are less able to retain moisture.

☐ *Check when completed*

❧ TIP 304 ❧

Know before you sow! Slightly dampen paper towels and lay them on a cookie sheet; arrange some old or questionable seeds (about an inch apart). Cover with a damp paper towel, encase the project in a plastic bag, and set in a warm place (at least 65 degrees Fahrenheit). Check back in a few days; ideally at least half should have sprouted.

❑ *Check when completed*

❧ TIP 305 ❧

Inventory and clean your
pot collection. New ones are not
cheap, and it's easy to get the old
ones back into shape. First, scrape
out any residue. Soak very dirty pots
in a tub or scrub them with a
sponge. Finally, sterilize everything
in a diluted bleach solution
(1 part bleach to 10 parts water)
and air-dry.

☐ *Check when completed*

❧ TIP 306 ❧

Tune up your hand tools. With a
damp rag, wipe metal surfaces
clean of last year's encrusted dirt,
caked-on sap, or other crud (or soak
or chip it away). Use coarse
sandpaper or steel wool to sand off
rust spots. Finally, wipe all
blades clean with a rag soaked in
linseed oil (or substitute vegetable
oil from your kitchen).

❑ *Check when completed*

❧ TIP 307 ❧

Review new plant information in the gardening magazines. These annual roundups usually appear in the January or February issue of all major publications and are great fun to read and dream over. Here you can learn about a brand-new, disease-resistant rose or a good, new short-season hot pepper.

❑ *Check when completed*

❧ TIP 308 ❧

Stop using traditional road salt on
your driveway, steps, and walk-
ways. Some may run off into the
road, but plenty can seep into your
soil. Its presence inhibits roots
from absorbing water. Trees and
shrubs can develop brown (dead)
growth; flowerbeds may be
contaminated; and salt often harms
a lawn. Instead, use sand.

❑ *Check when completed*

❧ TIP 309 ❧

Check indoor gift plants, like pretty potted azaleas, for insect pests. The dry heat of a home in winter often leads to outbreaks of tiny red spider mites, which form cobwebs and congregate on the bottoms of leaves. Put the pot in the sink and spray thoroughly with stiff jets of water. Repeat, if needed, in a few days.

❑ *Check when completed*

❧ TIP 310 ❧

Time to shop! Gather all your
current seed catalogs. Then cruise
through them with a pack of
yellow sticky notes, flagging pages
with items you want. Compare
similar varieties and look for new
items. Compare prices, check
shipping charges, and make a wish
list. Then pare down the list
to fit your budget.

❑ *Check when completed*

✤ TIP 311 ✤

Check on stored vegetables such as
onions, garlic, and winter squash.
They should be in a cool—but not
freezing—dark place such as the
basement or mudroom. Pull out
and discard any that have sprouted,
have soft spots, or are starting to
rot. They won't be good to eat,
plus the problem could spread.

☐ *Check when completed*

❧ TIP 312 ❧

Brown or rotted spots on your
African violet leaves? Check to be
sure that you have not overwatered.
There should be no water in their
saucers 20 minutes after watering.

The best way to water African
violets is from the bottom. Just set
the pot in a saucer of water and let
the plant wick up what it needs,
discarding any remaining water.

❑ *Check when completed*

❧ TIP 313 ❧

This may be your Year of the Rose!
Check out the All-America Rose
Selections winners; results are
announced in newspaper gardening
columns and winter issues of
gardening magazines (or you can
visit *www.aars.org*). Thumb
through a good book on the topic
by an expert, such as *A Year of
Roses* by Stephen Scanniello.

❏ *Check when completed*

❧ TIP 314 ❧

Order your seeds—for flowers, as
well as vegetables—sooner rather
than later. Mail-order seed
companies get very busy in the
next month or so, and early
orders are fulfilled faster. Plus you
are more likely to get exactly
what you want, with no
substitutions or rainchecks.

❑ *Check when completed*

❧ TIP 315 ❧

Plan your flowerbeds on paper.
Make yourself do this before you
peek at the nursery catalogs, so you
don't "put the cart before
the horse." Your plan may be an
informal picture on regular or
graph paper, but try to make it
to scale. Gardening books and
nursery catalogs will help you
estimate mature-plant sizes.

❏ *Check when completed*

❧ TIP 316 ❧

Amaryllis plant all done blooming?
Pinch off the fading flowers before
the plant expends too much energy
trying to go to seed. Move the
plant to a sunny window; continue
to water it and lightly feed it. The
more and healthier leaves it has, the
more flower stalks it will be able
to generate next winter.

❏ *Check when completed*

❧ TIP 317 ❧

Do your favorite houseplants suddenly have dry edges or brown leaf tips? Low humidity is the culprit, a common problem this time of year. There are several ways to bring them relief: Spritz them occasionally; place them on a tray or dish of pebbles so runoff water can evaporate around them; or place plants closer together.

❑ *Check when completed*

❧ TIP 318 ❧

It's time to stock up on basic seed-starting supplies! You need shallow flats and small pots with drainage holes in the bottoms, labels, several bags of sterile soilless potting mix (available right now at home-supply stores and garden centers), and some plastic wrap for temporary coverings.

❏ *Check when completed*

❦ TIP 319 ❦

Decide where you'd like to keep
your developing seedlings, and
prepare or clear out the area.
Choose a warm area free of drafts. If
there is no or poor light, you can
provide artificial light. Fluorescent is
better than ordinary light bulbs, or
you can buy "grow lights." Set lights
to be adjustable, so they are kept only
inches above seedlings as they grow.

☐ *Check when completed*

❖ TIP 320 ❖

Check the birdfeeders out in the
yard. Damp or snowy weather can
cause birdseed to clump and rot.
You may have to empty out the
whole feeder, wipe it clean with
paper towels, and refill with fresh
seed. The chickadees, especially,
will appreciate your efforts.

❑ *Check when completed*

❧ TIP 321 ❧

Join a plant society. For modest dues, this is a great way to get information and meet others who share your enthusiasm for a certain type of plant. Benefits may also include regular meetings, plant swaps, plant shows with awards, and helpful publications. To find one, scan the classified ads of gardening magazines or search the Internet.

❑ *Check when completed*

❖ TIP 322 ❖

Prevent damping-off disease, a
fungus that attacks developing
seedlings, causing them to shrivel
and die right at soil level. The fungi
thrive in stagnant air and high
humidity. An ounce of prevention is
worth a pound of cure, so use clean
containers and a sterile, soilless
seed-starting mix.

❑ *Check when completed*

❧ TIP 323 ❧

Poinsettia still looking good? These popular holiday plants like about six hours of bright light each day. Avoid cold, drafty areas. Too much heat is bad for them, causing the color to fade and the leaves to fall off. Water regularly to keep the soil moist but not soggy, and prevent rot by emptying the saucer of excess water.

☐ *Check when completed*

❧ TIP 324 ❧

This is a fine time to repot your houseplants. They may be pot-bound, or the soil mix may be compacted or worn out. Your plants will repay you with a fresh surge of growth. Remember to accommodate special needs— African violets like a more peaty mix; succulents prefer extra sand or perlite for better drainage.

❏ *Check when completed*

❧ TIP 325 ❧

Make your own potting soil—it's fun and as easy as mixing cake batter! Spread newspapers over the work area. In a large bucket, mix by hand or with a trowel good ingredients such as loam or purified topsoil, peat moss, and sand or perlite. Mix equal parts or tailor your recipe to special plant needs.

❏ *Check when completed*

❧ TIP 326 ❧

Organize your garden magazines
(which by now may be in unread
piles). Group similar ones, in
chronological order, and put them
in binders or cases. Note that often-
times the December or January
issue contains an annual index,
which you might want to copy and
keep separate for quick reference.
Take your time—stop to read!

❑ *Check when completed*

❖ TIP 327 ❖

Does a favorite houseplant look
top-heavy and crowded? It could be
time to divide it. Ready a few new
pots and fresh potting soil. Run a
knife around the inside of the pot to
help dislodge the plant. Shake loose
soil off the roots. Then pry the
plant apart, with fingers or a sharp
knife, and repot each piece.

❑ *Check when completed*

❖ TIP 328 ❖

Have you ever seen those cacti that
are plain on the bottom but topped
with a different or colorful cactus?
You can make your own graft. Pick
plants similar in size. Cut with a
sharp, clean knife; fit the parts
together; and hold them in place
with a rubber band or two. They
should knit together in a few weeks.

❏ *Check when completed*

❧ TIP 329 ❧

Start flower seeds indoors in flats
or pots. Some require light to
germinate and must be laid on the
surface of a flat of seed-starting mix
or sand. Others can be covered
lightly. The seed packet will have
this information. Then place them
in a warm, draft-free spot.

❑ *Check when completed*

❖ TIP 330 ❖

Draw up a new plan for your
vegetable garden—and aim to
rotate crops. If you grow the same
thing in the same spot each year,
plant-specific pests will know it,
hang around, and re-attack, so you
want to confuse or thwart them.
Also, rotating crops keeps vital soil
nutrients from becoming depleted.

❑ *Check when completed*

❧ TIP 331 ❧

Planning a big project or instal-
lation this year, such as a new patio
or terrace, a water garden, or a
pergola? It's not too soon to start
researching the idea and getting
design ideas, from books, magazines, and the Internet. And if you
think you will need some help, line
up somebody right now—before
his or her calendar fills.

☐ *Check when completed*

❖ TIP 332 ❖

Inspect the yard for winter
damage. If a branch or limb is
obviously dead—snapped, dry, or
blackened—clip or saw it off. Make
your cuts flush with the branch
bark collar. If you are not sure that
a branch is dead, wait a few more
weeks. A dormant limb can look
dead but still have life in it.

❏ *Check when completed*

❖ TIP 333 ❖

Clean dusty houseplant leaves.
Not only is the coating unattractive,
but it inhibits the exchange of air
and moisture for the plant, which
can be bad for its health. Wipe
leaves with a soapy sponge, and
then rinse with clear water. Dust
and dirt can be brushed off textured
or fuzzy leaves with a paintbrush or
clean make-up brush.

❑ *Check when completed*

❖ TIP 334 ❖

Always water flats and pots of developing seeds from the bottom. Watering from above is too rough—the seeds are so small and fragile that they are easily knocked over or dislodged. Instead, set their container in a slightly larger one of water and let them slurp up the water they need.

❑ *Check when completed*

❧ TIP 335 ❧

Keep ice from forming on your garden pool. If the surface gets covered over completely, gases harmful to overwintering fish and plants become trapped. Luckily, all you have to do to prevent this is float a ball or block of wood in the water. It will bob about and maintain an opening even in freezing weather.

❏ *Check when completed*

❧ TIP 336 ❧

On a mild day, tour the yard and look closely for signs of frost heaving. Freeze-thaw cycles cause entire plant rootballs, especially of newer plants and shrubs, to rise above the ground, sometimes at alarmingly crooked angles. Just push the plants back into place, and mulch or remulch them to prevent it from happening again.

❑ *Check when completed*

❧ TIP 337 ❧

Find out your area's predicted last frost-free date. Check your local paper, or call a garden center or nearby Cooperative Extension office. Though it's usually not till April or May, depending where you live, you need to know now so you can calculate when to start certain seeds indoors—seeds you plan to set outside after the last frost.

❑ *Check when completed*

❧ TIP 338 ❧

Sharpen your cutting tools. This means pruners, clippers, and loppers, of course, but also shovels and hoes. Use a file and restore the original bevel. There is no need for a razor-sharp edge, just smooth the nicks. If the tool is unwieldy, hold it in place with a vise grip while you work. When finished, store the tools in a cool, dry place.

❑ *Check when completed*

❧ TIP 339 ❧

If you haven't done so already,
service your lawn mower. Clean off
the entire surface, above and below.
Then, drain the gas, change the oil,
and sharpen the blades before
returning the machine to storage.
You'll be congratulating yourself
for taking the time now when you
need it to be in top running
condition come spring.

☐ *Check when completed*

❧ TIP 340 ❧

Note weather and garden events
on your calendar or in your garden
journal. Record animal and bird
activities, as well as early signs of
plant life. If you get into this habit,
you'll find the information
really useful in the years to come,
when you are looking for patterns
or want to get an early start on
an outdoor project.

☐ *Check when completed*

❧ TIP 341 ❧

Have the seeds you started indoors begun to poke their heads up? When the first true set of leaves appears (technically the second set; the leaves look different from the first, lowest ones), use a small pair of sharp scissors to thin out smaller or weaker seedlings right at soil level.

❑ *Check when completed*

❧ TIP 342 ❧

Inventory your garden supplies to see whether you are running low on anything. Garden stores are already restocking, and though it seems a bit premature, there's no harm in going shopping now to get what you anticipate needing—pesticides, herbicides, fertilizers, soil amendments, stakes, plant labels, maybe even a new tool or two.

❏ *Check when completed*

❧ TIP 343 ❧

If your orchids aren't blooming,
or have inflorescences with buds
that haven't yet opened, the
wait can be excruciating. Nudge
things along by feeding the plants
once a month with orchid fertilizer
(diluted according to the label
directions). Raising the temperature
or humidity may also help,
depending on the type of orchid.

❑ *Check when completed*

❧ TIP 344 ❧

A sure cure for cabin fever
is a homemade terrarium. Any
good-sized glass container will do;
a former aquarium is perfect.
Spread an inch or two of slightly
damp sphagnum moss in the
bottom, top with sand, and plant
little plants. Ferns, baby's tears, and
peperomias are fine choices.

❏ *Check when completed*

❧ TIP 345 ❧

Pamper a Valentine's bouquet
of roses so it will last as long as
possible. To do this, prepare a vase
of lukewarm water and stir in the
preservative powder from the
florist. Then recut the stems on
an angle (to increase water uptake).
Set the arrangement in a cool room
overnight to plump up. Then
display in a bright room.

❑ *Check when completed*

❧ TIP 346 ❧

After a snowstorm, help your
hedges by brushing off the snow
with a broom. If you don't
do this, the weight may snap or kill
the branches. Sometimes, the
entire plant can get pushed askew
and will then look misshapen when
spring returns. Allow ice on the
stems to melt on its own.

❏ *Check when completed*

❧ TIP 347 ❧

Did you take photographs of
your garden last year? Now is a good
time to gather them, group
them by season, and maybe even put
them in a small album. Just
looking at them will cheer you up
on a wintry day and inspire new
ideas for the coming spring.

☐ *Check when completed*

❧ TIP 348 ❧

It's time to start some houseplant cuttings. Water the plant the night before. Cut young shoots, about 3 or 4 inches long, and dip their cut ends in hormone rooting powder (available at any garden supplier). Then stick them in a flat or pot of moist, sterile, soilless mix. Cover with plastic, and place in a warm spot.

❏ *Check when completed*

❖ TIP 349 ❖

Go shopping and treat yourself to a
new pair of gardening gloves! Try
them on first to be sure they are
comfortable and that you can move
your fingers and wrists easily. If
you are really in the mood to
splurge, get calfskin ones—they'll
serve you well for years to come.

❑ *Check when completed*

❧ TIP 350 ❧

Prepare your orders to mail-order
plant nurseries. Even if you are
phoning in the order, fill out
the order blank that comes with the
catalog so you'll have the product
code numbers and prices handy.
Read the fine print about shipping
costs and timing, and the replace-
or-refund policy, just in case.

❑ *Check when completed*

❧ TIP 351 ❧

Those seedlings you've been raising in flats may be ready to move to the next step. Fill individual pots with moistened, sterile potting mix. Then carefully transplant the seedlings to the pots. Set these in a bright spot, or better still, provide around fourteen hours a day of artificial light.

❑ *Check when completed*

❧ TIP 352 ❧

Check on all your developing
seedlings. Remember to water
before feeding, or at the same time,
so the roots can take up the
nutrients. If the seedlings are
leaning towards the light source,
move the pots a quarter turn
each day to encourage the
stems to grow upright.

❑ *Check when completed*

❧ TIP 353 ❧

Start some perennials from
seeds (purchased locally or via
mail-order). A few that sprout and
grow readily are hollyhocks, phlox,
and mums. Now is a good time to
find some new colors in these
common plants—seed houses tend
to have broader selections than
you'll see later in the spring
at the garden center.

❏ *Check when completed*

❧ TIP 354 ❧

If you're growing Lenten roses, also
called by their Latin name,
Helleborus, they may be starting to
poke up their heads, snow or not.
Check that they are not being
smothered by mulch or snow, and
pinch off tattered growth to make
way for new stems and leaves—and
soon, those glorious flowers.

❑ *Check when completed*

❖ TIP 355 ❖

Did you have any leftover bulbs
when you planted last fall? You
might try potting them now.
Give them a little water and
warmth, and some indirect light. If
you're lucky, they'll oblige by
sprouting. Pots of blooming bulbs
offer such cheer around the house
on gray winter days.

❑ *Check when completed*

❧ TIP 356 ❧

Stop by the garden center to see whether they are unloading the last of the paper-white narcissus and amaryllis bulbs. You may get a real deal, and there's no reason you can't bring them home, pot them, and get them growing. There's still lots of time to enjoy their unique beauty (and in the case of the paper-whites, wonderful fragrance).

❑ *Check when completed*

✦ TIP 357 ✦

Want some free shrubs and trees? It's not hard to propagate your own from hardwood cuttings started this time of year. Take slender pieces of stem about a foot long. Prepare flats or bags of vermiculite (available at garden centers), and store the cuttings, cut side down, until spring.

☐ *Check when completed*

❧ TIP 358 ❧

Some of your bushes and
trees, as well as your roses, may
have suckers emerging from
the roots. (Rose suckers are below
the graft.) These are easier to spot
this time of year. Cut them off
cleanly at ground level with sharp
loppers so they never have a chance
to start growing and stealing energy
from the main plant.

❑ *Check when completed*

❖ TIP 359 ❖

Start cool-weather vegetables such as broccoli and its relatives. These need time to become sturdy seedlings so they can be the first ones out into the garden when winter is over but before hot weather arrives (they do poorly in hot weather). Try to start them six to eight weeks before you plan to transplant.

❏ *Check when completed*

❖ TIP 360 ❖

Expand your resource
base by adding a book to your
library. Cool Springs Press
specializes in state and regional
gardening books. Visit
www.coolspringspress.net
or check out the list in the
back of this book!

❏ *Check when completed*

❖ APPENDIX ❖

PLANT INVENTORY/HISTORY

name _____
when planted _____
where planted _____
size _____
source _____
price _____

name _____
when planted _____
where planted _____
size _____
source _____
price _____

PLANT INVENTORY/HISTORY

name _____

when planted _____

where planted _____

size _____

source _____

price _____

name _____

when planted _____

where planted _____

size _____

source _____

price _____

PLANT INVENTORY/HISTORY

name _____

when planted _____

where planted _____

size _____

source _____

price _____

name _____

when planted _____

where planted _____

size _____

source _____

price _____

PLANT INVENTORY/HISTORY

name _____

when planted _____

where planted _____

size _____

source _____

price _____

name _____

when planted _____

where planted _____

size _____

source _____

price _____

PLANT INVENTORY/HISTORY

name _____

when planted _____

where planted _____

size _____

source _____

price _____

name _____

when planted _____

where planted _____

size _____

source _____

price _____

PLANT INVENTORY/HISTORY

name _____

when planted _____

where planted _____

size _____

source _____

price _____

name _____

when planted _____

where planted _____

size _____

source _____

price _____

TODAY IN MY GARDEN

_____
_____
_____
_____
_____
_____
_____
_____
_____
_____

TODAY IN MY GARDEN

_____
_____
_____
_____
_____
_____
_____
_____
_____
_____
_____

TODAY IN MY GARDEN

TODAY IN MY GARDEN

My Favorite Sources

My Favorite Sources

Other Great Books

Month-by-Month Gardening Series in: **ISBN**

FROM COOL SPRINGS PRESS!

Gardener's Guide Series in: **ISBN**

Mid-Atlantic. 1-93060-499-8

New England 1-93060-449-1

New Jersey 1-59186-067-9

New York 1-59186-065-2

Pennsylvania. 1-93060-479-3

And that's not all; visit **www.coolspringspress.net** to read about
some of our other books!

Managing Editor: Billie Brownell
Cover and Interior Design: Bruce Gore, Gore Studios
Tip Writer: Teri Dunn
Production Design: S.E. Anderson